1987

Ethics and Nuclear Arms

Ethics and Nuclear Arms

European and American Perspectives

Edward R. Norman ● Richard John Neuhaus
Wolfhart Pannenberg ● J. Bryan Hehir
Frans Alting von Geusau ● Michael Novak
Stephen Haseler ● Sven F. Kraemer
Erwin Wilkens ● Robert A. Gessert

Edited by Raymond English
Foreword by Paul H. Nitze

Ethics and Public Policy Center
Washington, D.C.

Library of Congress Cataloging in Publication Data
Main entry under title:
Ethics and nuclear arms.
  Bibliography: p.
  Includes index.
  1. Nuclear warfare—Moral and ethical aspects—
Addresses, essays, lectures. 2. Nuclear warfare—
Religious aspects—Christianity—Addresses, essays,
lectures. I. Norman, Edward R. II. English, Raymond.
III. Ethics and Public Policy Center (Washington, D.C.)
U263.E82   1985   174′.42   85-10304
ISBN 0-89633-095-8

$7.00

Contents

Foreword

PAUL H. NITZE

SINCE THE END of the Second World War, American—as well as world—opinion has tended to focus on one major foreign policy issue at a time. In the late 1940s, the issue was Berlin and access to that divided city; in the early 1950s, Korea; in the early 1960s, Cuba. In the latter half of the 1960s and early 1970s the issue was Vietnam.

Today's focal issue, both here and abroad, is nuclear arms control. Arms control is not an end in itself but a means. The object of arms-control negotiations is to support foreign policy and security policy by negotiating agreements that will contribute to reducing the risk of war, primarily nuclear war. Other purposes—stopping the arms race, saving money, increasing stability, assuring predictability, providing the foundation for a better East-West relationship—may well be desirable, but only if they contribute to the more important goal of reducing the risk of war and strengthening the prospects of peace.

American policymakers during the late 1940s hoped that the use of force in international affairs, or even the threat of using force, could be avoided. But just as, in assuring internal tranquility, the resort to force cannot be wholly avoided, so also, in support of order in international affairs, deterrence through the threat of force and on occasion the actual use of force cannot be avoided. A government's use of force, whether internationally or internally, should be based on principle and on a process that gives it legitimacy.

Let us assume, for the moment, that there is in fact a consensus, not only in the United States but in the rest of the world not controlled by Moscow, in support of peace, international stability, and order. What then should be the proximate aim of policy?

I suggest that the key phrase describing the aim of our policy should be "live and let live." The Soviet phrase "peaceful coexistence" means exactly that to non-Communist ears. This is not the meaning Khrushchev and Brezhnev gave it, but for once let us take a phrase of theirs and give it the meaning we believe it should have. Moscow in the past, when the West was united and strong, has accommodated to the literal meaning. If we regain a relatively clear and united view of the basic purposes of policy, we can accomplish much.

The ten essays in this book shed light on the real problems facing us as we try to reduce the risk of war and strengthen the prospects of peace. Reflecting both European and American perspectives, both Protestant and Catholic points of view, the writers ponder the ethics of possessing and using nuclear weapons. They disagree over details and differ in emphases; yet they reflect a remarkable consensus about the political necessity and moral legitimacy of the Western alliance. The Ethics and Public Policy Center has performed a noteworthy service in organizing a series of seminars on these questions and publishing the resulting papers. I commend this collection to policymakers, educators, and concerned citizens.

Serious discussion of nuclear arms is essential if we are to avoid nuclear war and reduce the stockpiles of these weapons. We owe it to our children, our grandchildren—and to my great-grandchild—to hold out for some brighter vision for the future.

Preface

D URING THE LATE 1970S the countries of Western Europe came under a new threat. Until then there had been a nuclear stand-off in Europe, built upon the mutual threat of intercontinental-range missiles (ICBMs) targeted mainly on the USSR and the USA, together with the possible use of short-range, low-yield tactical nuclear arms. For more than thirty years these weapons systems had kept the peace and preserved the independence of the Western European states in the face of the Warsaw Pact's superiority in conventional forces and Moscow's unyielding commitment to world hegemony.

But after 1976 there was a new factor in the strategic equation. The Soviet Union started to deploy intermediate-range nuclear missiles, targeted on military installations and cities from Oslo to Istanbul. Some SS-20s were also directed against China and could reach the Pacific rimland. Their flight-time was considerably less than that of ICBMs and their accuracy greater. Each missile carried three nuclear warheads (multiple independently targetable re-entry vehicles, or MIRVs) with a range of 5,000 kilometers. By 1979, nearly 800 intermediate-range warheads were in place.

The deployment of the Soviet SS-20s meant that NATO's nuclear deterrent was no longer fully credible, and Western Europe was vulnerable to nuclear blackmail. If the Warsaw Pact powers were to invade Western Europe with conventional forces and threaten to use SS-20s on ports, airfields, and industrial areas, the Western powers, having no intermediate-range missiles, would have no equivalent deterrent.

This was the predicament that led to NATO's 1979 decision to deploy intermediate-range American nuclear missiles—Pershing IIs and Ground Launched Cruise Missiles—in Western Europe. But Washington and its allies agreed not to deploy these weapons if the

Soviet Union withdrew its SS-20s out of range of Western European targets.

The NATO decision triggered extraordinary protest, and a new "peace" movement was launched throughout Western Europe and in North America. Its aim was to prevent deployment of the Western counterparts to the Soviet SS-20s, that is, to leave the Warsaw bloc with the strategic advantage and the possibility of nuclear blackmail against Western Europe. The Soviet Union, both openly and through KGB channels, enthusiastically supported the Western "peace" movement.

Many churches in Europe and America became involved in the nuclear debate. The Synod of the Church of England, despite much pressure from the peace movement, decided to support a continued policy of deterrence. The Catholic bishops in Germany, the Netherlands, France, and the United States issued pastoral statements on nuclear arms, ranging from an ambiguous condemnation of nuclear deterrence in the American pastoral letter to an affirmation of deterrent policies by the German and French bishops. The World Council of Churches, meeting at Vancouver, Canada, in August 1983, issued a blanket condemnation of nuclear weapons and nuclear deterrence. Many representatives of organized religion spoke of the need to renounce policies of nuclear deterrence in order to save the human race.

To encourage thoughtful theological and ethical analysis of the current state of nuclear arms and nuclear deterrence, the Ethics and Public Policy Center organized three seminars for religious leaders from Europe and America. Co-sponsors of the two seminars held in Europe were: in Britain (May 1983), the Institute for European Defence and Strategic Studies; and in the Netherlands (September 1983), the Stichting Vredes Politiek (SVP) and the Interchurch Committee for Bilateral Disarmament (ICTO). The third seminar took place in Washington in October 1983.

The ten essays presented in this volume are drawn from papers given at these seminars. In the first essay, British scholar Stephen Haseler traces the history of the nuclear arms issue and suggests why it moved to center stage in 1983. In the second, a White House expert on arms control, Sven F. Kraemer, explains the nuclear-arms and arms-control policy of the Reagan administration.

The next three essays are by Protestants: Erwin Wilkens, a leader of the German Evangelical Church (Lutheran), and theologian Wolfhart Pannenberg examine the debate in German churches over nuclear arms. An American Lutheran theologian, Richard John Neuhaus, relates the question in U.S. churches to their crisis of faith.

Three Catholics speak next. Father J. Bryan Hehir, chief advisor to the U.S. bishops on war and peace, interprets the bishops' 1983 pastoral letter on nuclear arms. Catholic scholar and commentator Michael Novak suggests that the bishops labored under an inadequate view of the nature of the Soviet threat. Dutch professor Frans A. M. Alting von Geusau examines nuclear pacifism and the true meaning of peace in today's world.

Robert A. Gessert, a defense expert who is also a clergyman in the United Church of Christ, focuses on the need for NATO to confront the "first use" question: Can there be a controlled, limited, morally acceptable use of nuclear weapons to counter an unprovoked non-nuclear attack?

Finally, Cambridge historian Edward R. Norman, an Anglican priest, looks at the historical Christian view of war and peace and its meaning in the nuclear age.

At the end of 1983 the deployment of American intermediate-range missiles began according to schedule. With the first missiles in place the "peace" agitation subsided, and Soviet active support for the movement apparently subsided also.

The debate over the morality of nuclear deterrence continues, however, with varying intensity. So does the debate over how best to prevent World War III. As these lines are written, the debate turns largely on the feasibility and justification of strategic defense against nuclear missiles—President Reagan's Strategic Defense Initiative. It is complicated by the resumption of nuclear-arms-control negotiations and by the deployment of yet another Soviet missile: the fifth-generation SS-X-24 ICBM, which may prove to be the first completely mobile and elusive land-based strategic missile. Technology takes unpredictable turns, but the ethical criteria for defensive measures do not change.

In publishing these essays, we remember with affection, gratitude, and sorrow one whose enthusiastic support was indispensable in planning the seminars, and whose death within days after the final one cast a shadow over all who knew him. Wilhelm F. Bofinger, a high official of the Evangelische Kirche in West Germany, was the beloved pastor of the German Lutheran Community in Washington, D.C., from 1973 to 1983. He saw the defense of freedom, justice, and peace as a central concern for Christians in our time, and he was indefatigable in his efforts to bring together men and women of good will on both sides of the Atlantic in thoughtful dialogue. To Pastor Bofinger's memory this book is affectionately dedicated.

RAYMOND ENGLISH, *Vice President*
Ethics and Public Policy Center

Washington, D.C.
June 5, 1985

Four Decades With Nuclear Arms

STEPHEN HASELER

WHY DID THE QUESTION of nuclear arms move in from its peripheral status to become one of the central issues of our time? It was never unimportant, of course. But it did not in previous decades arouse the passions, engage the intellects, or divide the polities of the West in the way that it does today.

The momentous decision of President Truman in 1945 to use nuclear weapons did not set in train a great national or international soul-searching. Certainly there was an undercurrent of controversy over this grave decision, and certainly the bombings of Hiroshima and Nagasaki became fixed in the public memory as a warning of the horror of nuclear war. Yet, for reasons that are not difficult to fathom, Truman's decision did not bring about the intense division of opinion that the Vietnam conventional conflict of a later period created. The acquisition of nuclear weapons by other powers (the Soviet Union, Britain, France) also occurred without serious internal political division. To this day, France, the third-ranking nuclear power, has no serious unilateralist or nuclear pacifist movement.

After the war, though there were disputes over the details of nuclear doctrine, there was little domestic opposition in the United States to the development of a nuclear defensive system. The government for twenty years and more had a seemingly unbreakable domestic consensus behind its nuclear policy. When Dean Acheson said he was "present at the creation," he was referring to the creation of a Western security system that has had more sustained popular support than any other Western global strategy in this century.

Stephen Haseler is professor of government at the City of London Polytechnic and the author or co-author of six books and numerous articles. He was a founding member of the Social Democratic party of the United Kingdom and is a former deputy mayor of Greater London.

1

In the United Kingdom, it was the Labour government of Clement Attlee and Ernest Bevin that decided to embark upon an independent nuclear deterrent and to lead the Western European nations into NATO—a defensive pact that from its inception was explicitly based on the threatened use of nuclear weapons. This decision was supported by the Conservative party, not surprisingly, but also widely on the British left and by, among others, the *New Statesman and Nation*. During the 1950s and 1960s, as the arms race—by which is normally meant the nuclear arms race—increased, it rarely touched off the kind of intellectual agony and political divisions now apparent.

Surviving the Cold War

The consensus about the need for the West both to possess nuclear weapons and to construct an alliance based upon the threat of their use survived all the vicissitudes and tensions of the Cold War years. Even the Cuban missile crisis of 1962, when a super-power confrontation seemed to bring the world nearer to global conflict than ever before, could not shake the massive Western consensus behind its nuclear weapons policy.

Of course, from the dawning of the nuclear age there has always been a strain of nuclear pacifist sentiment in Western societies—a belief that Western governments should not in any circumstances even threaten to use nuclear weapons. (Although nuclear pacifism is by no means the same as conventional pacifism, many nuclear pacifists do not support a "compensating" buildup of conventional arms should the West disarm in a nuclear sense.) Yet nuclear pacifism remained an underground stream for thirty years after 1945. The pacifism that pervaded much of Europe during the 1930s did not transform itself into nuclear pacifism in the obviously more dangerous world of the late 1940s through 1960s. What underpinned the pacifism of the 1930s was a collective memory of World War I.   . Arguably, what underpinned deterrence in more recent decades was the failure of pacifism in the 1930s.

During the Cold War years, no major political party in the Western democracies (with one exception, which I will mention shortly) even flirted with the notion of nuclear pacifism or unilateral nuclear disarmament. American liberals and conservatives, Democrats and

Republicans; British Labourites and Conservatives; West German Christian Democrats, Free Democrats, and Social Democrats; Italian Christian Democrats and most Italian Socialist factions; French rightists, Gaullists, and Socialists—all accepted in various forms a Western or national defense based upon the threat of the use of nuclear weapons.

The one exception occurred in my own country. During 1959-60, the British Campaign for Nuclear Disarmament, then as now largely a middle-class movement, under the leadership of Bertrand Russell and Canon Lewis Collins managed to persuade the opposition Labour party to adopt a unilateralist posture. Labour pledged to reject a defense policy based upon the possibility of using nuclear weapons. This pledge was overturned by the party conference the following year, and Aneurin Bevan, then leader of the left faction within the Labour party, referred to this interlude as a "spasm." For fifteen years after that Labour did not even review its policy of supporting nuclear deterrence.

Another intriguing aspect of the history of the nuclear issue is that the Western consensus behind nuclear deterrence survived the political radicalism and intellectual counter-establishmentarianism of the 1960s. Nuclear pacifism was but a minor element in the political radicalism that infused the left during this period. In the United States and Western Europe, Vietnam, not the nuclear posture of NATO, became the central issue. And in Western Europe, even the most extreme manifestation of political opposition to Western society, "Eurocommunism," was forced, as it temporarily glimpsed power, to make many concessions to the overwhelming public support for NATO and its nuclear defense posture. The great defense debates of the sixties were over questions of nuclear doctrine and strategy—"Mutual Assured Destruction," flexible and limited response, detailed matters of arms control, and the like — rather than about the validity of nuclear deterrence.

Breakdown of the Consensus

Today the situation is radically different. Nuclear pacifism has, at least in Western Europe, broken out of its esoteric mold and become an important political movement. Nuclear pacifism will not, as it did in 1961, disappear like a snowflake in early spring. In a peculiar geographic reversal, it is in northern rather than southern Europe that nuclear pacifist sentiments are now most firmly ensconced. The British Labour party and large sections of the British Liberal party are in favor of unilateral nuclear disarmament—eliminating Britain's independent nuclear force and expelling America's nuclear presence from British soil and waters. In West Germany the Social Democratic party, once the bastion of NATO sympathies, is against deployment of the cruise and Pershing II missiles on German soil. But it has to contend for the anti-nuclear constituency with the Green party, now seated in the Bundestag. Not since the founding of the West German republic has opinion been so divided. The Dutch position, as far as it can be understood, is one of awaiting developments but with no firm commitment to deploy the weapons.

What all this amounts to is that the political consensus behind the West's nuclear posture has broken down. Contradictory positions about nuclear weapons and defense policy are often held, and with passionate intensity. Polling data substantiate a discernible growth of neutralist sentiment since the mid-1970s. When asked whether Western Europe would be safer if it moved toward neutralism, European publics responded in a rather alarming fashion. The percentages supporting such a move were 57 per cent in West Germany, 53 in the Netherlands, 45 in Great Britain, and 43 in France. At the same time, the percentages that favored remaining in NATO, a defense alliance specifically based upon nuclear weapons, were 64 per cent in West Germany, 59 in Great Britain, 56 in the Netherlands, and 33 in France (a figure that reflects France's historically ambivalent position towards NATO).

There is also a division in Europe between ordinary public opinion and elite opinion about the United States. The general public in the European countries continues to like and admire the United States and to believe it is committed to European security. But higher-status Western Europeans have come to distrust U.S. judgment and leadership, particularly in defense.

Yet nuclear pacifism is still a decidedly minority position throughout Western Europe and is likely to remain so. The 1983 election victories of Mrs. Thatcher and Chancellor Kohl took place in a political environment in which nuclear defense in alliance with the United States was the overriding issue.

The New Factor: Fear

A point to keep in mind is that nuclear pacifism is not the same as neutralism. There are Western European neutralists or quasi-neutralists, many of them on the right and bitterly anti-Soviet, who envisage a nuclear defense for Europe divorced from that of the United States. This nuclear defense would be either multilateral—a combination of British and French forces—or national. I believe, however, that both unilateralism (i.e., the advocacy of unilateral nuclear disarmament) and neutralism, as well as the nuclear freeze movement in the United States, are the products of a new factor in world politics—a fear of nuclear war.

This emotion has a powerful hold on many Europeans, and on some Americans. A colleague of mine in London, Philip Towle, quoted Europe's leading unilateralist guru, E. P. Thompson, as saying that "if the European NATO states, under popular pressure, should reject cruise missiles and Pershing IIs, and if the Soviet Union did not instantly hold that they would reduce their SS-20s, we can be sure that the Western unilateralist movement would at once lose its popular support." To this Dr. Towle replied: "Actually, we can be sure of no such thing, since Western unilateralism is based upon the fear of nuclear war, and the more intransigently the Soviet Union behaves, the greater the fear of war." Despite the outrage exhibited by the world's public following the shooting down of the Korean civilian airliner in September 1983, the net result was only that the Soviet Union increased its reputation for resolve and intransigence.

This new fear of nuclear war is not, in my view, a result of the actual existence of nuclear weapons. After all, the peoples of the world have been living with nuclear stockpiles and delivery systems for three decades. The arsenals on both sides are now frighteningly high, but the potential for destruction in any general nuclear exchange was surely just as horrifying in the 1950s and 1960s as it is now.

Moreover, the new fear of war does not, in my view, stem from a new moral sensibility about nuclear weapons, a moral concern that was absent or stunted in the 1950s and 1960s. Nor can it be explained as a response to NATO nuclear strategy. The "first use" doctrine in the European theater has been NATO policy for over thirty years, though it is now being questioned for the first time by eminent men and women on both sides of the Atlantic.

The new fear of war cannot be attributed, either, to a supposed heightening of East-West tensions. To be sure, the advent of the Reagan administration made some Europeans a bit jittery, but President Reagan's rhetoric (which seems to cause more offense than his actions) has certainly been no more robust than that of candidate John F. Kennedy when he was running on the "missile gap" issue, or when, as president, he spoke of opposing any foe and aiding any friend in the defense of liberty. President Reagan's actions (Grenada notwithstanding) can hardly be called more confrontational than Dulles's "brinkmanship," Kennedy's reaction to the missiles in Cuba, LBJ's invasion of the Dominican Republic, or Eisenhower's massive troop landings in Lebanon.

If the new fear of war is not a product of the actual existence of nuclear weapons, or of a new moral sensibility, or of heightened East-West tensions, then what is the cause? My contention is that the new fear and the consequent intense debate about nuclear weapons are linked to a perceived instability in the power balance between East and West on the European continent. In the 1950s and 1960s the United States possessed nuclear superiority. This induced a sense of stability. Even as we entered the phase of "near parity" or "rough equivalence" in nuclear strategic arsenals in the 1970s, the essential stability of the balance was not, in my view, upset.

General De Gaulle thought otherwise. He believed that America's loss of nuclear superiority was of historic importance, the hinge of fate—that the United States, with its home population now hostage to the vagaries of a European conflict, could never be trusted to come to the aid of a Europe *in extremis*. De Gaulle is quoted as saying, on leaving office in 1969: "It is [the United States'] desire, and it will be satisfied one day, to desert Europe, you will see."

The Loss of Political Will

Yet the loss of American nuclear superiority is not what caused the widespread view that the balance of power in Europe had broken down. The crucial factor was not military hardware but the breakdown of political will, which was connected with the loss of American prestige following Vietnam, the oil crisis of 1973, the neutron weapon debacle, and the Iranian hostage situation, to cite the most obvious elements. In other words, along with the change in the nuclear balance from American superiority to near parity, the national consensus behind U.S. foreign policy—a consensus that had lasted through four post-war presidents—eroded. Two decades after its debut on the world stage as the first peacetime superpower, the United States appeared to lose the domestic where-withal to sustain this responsibility. The torch it had so firmly grasped when the British left Greece and Turkey in 1947 was hardly flickering when, under the impact of the Tet offensive, President Johnson decided to retire. The new American foreign policy chiefs, President Nixon and Dr. Kissinger, soon concluded that the flame had perhaps been extinguished altogether.

In his profound and impressive retrospective on the years following 1968, *The White House Years*, Dr. Kissinger expresses his anguish over the predicament of his country in this fateful period. "The fact remained that at the end of twenty years of exertion America was not at peace with itself," he wrote. "The consensus which had sustained our foreign policy had evaporated."

Kissinger also says that the world had changed significantly, superpower relationships had altered, and the United States needed to understand "the limits of power." The notion of "bipolarity" had given way to "multipolarity." The same arguments were heard from another part of the American political spectrum also. George Ball, a liberal internationalist who was an undersecretary of state during the 1960s, also prescribed a reduced role for the United States in a powerfully argued 1968 book entitled *The Discipline of Power*. Never before was impotence so roundly trumpeted.

Caught in a Double Bind

The West found itself in a double bind, a kind of geopolitical Catch-22. The loss of the stable bipolar world of the 1950s and 1960s caused concern, a concern that enhanced the fear of war. Yet any attempt to restore the *status quo ante* would itself cause an increase of anxiety and the fear of war. This was the daunting problem that faced the hapless President Carter in his last two years (after he realized the problem), and has also faced President Reagan. It was at the heart of the Intermediate-range Nuclear Force (INF) issue in

Europe in the winter of 1983-84. The attempt, initiated by West German chancellor Helmut Schmidt, to restore the theater nuclear weapons balance in Europe following the rapid Soviet buildup of SS-20s was an example of the problem—the need to restore a sense of security through a return to a previous condition even though the attempt to do so in itself increased anxiety.

Western leaders are faced with two rather stark alternatives. First, they can refuse to attempt to return to the stable bipolar world where American perceived power and will matched Soviet perceived power and will. Then the United States will continue to be seen as the weakening power in the world, while the Soviet Union is seen as the ascending power. This entails a political dynamic that is not only unfavorable to the West but deeply, perhaps cataclysmically, destabilizing.

Alternatively, the West can attempt to restore the bipolar balance, both militarily and in political will. In my view, this is the underlying task and opportunity represented by the INF deployment.

Ironically, the growth of nuclear pacifism demonstrates the validity of deterrence theory and the notion that stability and peace derive from an effective balance of power. The breakdown of this balance is, in my view, the reason why nuclear weapons have suddenly assumed a central position in the debate about peace and war, and why so many churchmen and theologians who had previously not entered the debate now seem compelled to do so.

Those who are now grappling with these momentous issues should bear in mind the asymmetry in the world on questions of ethics and nuclear armaments. A free and fruitful debate rages in the West; no similar debate occurs in the East. As Scott Thompson has noted, "General-Major Milovidov pointed out in 1980, 'Marxists-Leninists decisively reject the assertions of certain bourgeois theoreticians who consider nuclear missile war unjust from any point of view.' "[*]

For the first three decades of the nuclear age the world enjoyed relative stability. The vast majority in the West supported deterrence, and the defense of Western society and its values involved

---

[*]W. Scott Thompson, *Reducing Risk by Restoring Strength* (Washington: Ethics and Public Policy Center, 1983).

neither war nor surrender. There is no reason why this state of affairs—neither war nor surrender—cannot continue so long as deterrence remains effective.

This assertion cannot be proved. But the fact that deterrence worked so well for forty years ought to say something profound— if only that nuclear pacifism is too risky to supplant a tried and tested policy. Our task for the future, in the absence of multilateral nuclear disarmament (the preferred course of all sane men and women), is to make deterrence even more effective.

Toward a
Responsible Policy

SVEN F. KRAEMER

N UCLEAR ARMS-CONTROL POLICY involves profound ethical issues,
not merely technical or political problems. From the outset,
we need to understand that its serious dilemmas have no easy
answers, either ethical, technical, or diplomatic. There is no ready
"cure" available today that will simply and safely eliminate nuclear
arms, or any other weapons, from the world. The path toward such
goals is a difficult one with many pitfalls.

We must start with the paradox that in a world in which several
countries possess nuclear weapons, the United States needs to *have*
such weapons so that it will not need to *use* them—i.e., to prevent
nuclear war. Such nuclear deterrence has worked for more than
three decades.

In addition, we must recognize that a number of important American efforts to reduce nuclear arms risks have not been reciprocated
by the other global superpower, the Soviet Union. These include
the Baruch Plan of 1946 to put nuclear weapons under international
control, a proposal the Soviet Union rejected. Then there is the fact
that the United States greatly restricted its own strategic-force
modernization even as the Soviet Union accelerated the buildup of
its strategic forces. Similarly, the United States reduced its nuclear
arsenal in the past twenty years by more than one-fourth in numbers

Sven F. Kraemer is director of arms control on President Reagan's National
Security Council (NSC) staff. He joined the U.S. government in the Kennedy
administration and previously served with the NSC staff during the Johnson,
Nixon, and Ford administrations. He has a special interest in the ethical
dimensions and dilemmas of foreign and defense policy. This essay is based
on a lecture delivered in late 1983, and some of its figures may be slightly out
of date. However, while it is a personal, not an official, statement, Mr.
Kraemer's essay reflects policy considerations of the Reagan administration
in both its first and its second term. Some of the charts include information
through 1984, and a postscript carries the essay forward to April 1985. The
charts are at the end of the essay, pages 45–51.

of weapons and by some three-fourths in nuclear megatonnage. And now, during the administration of President Reagan, the United States at the U.S.-Soviet negotiations in Geneva has proposed additional deep cuts, especially in strategic and intermediate-range nuclear arms. But the Soviet Union has not yet agreed to deep reductions or to a number of other concrete measures proposed by the United States that could help reduce the nuclear danger and build confidence and trust.

The ethical dimension offers standards of judgment and grounds for hope and for continued effort that are not found in other approaches to the nuclear arms dilemma. We have to consider, first, what are the *right objectives* and criteria for effectively reducing the threat of nuclear war; second, what are the *most salient facts* about the historical context and current realities of arms-reduction efforts; and third, how *best* we can combine the right objectives with sobering realities to make a dangerous situation truly less dangerous. In this process, we must learn from history and avoid falling for simple short-term "solutions" that are built on illusions. We must instead work with sound knowledge by sound means for sound ends.

One example of a purported "cure" for nuclear weapons is the proposal currently fashionable in the United States for a "freeze" on the production, testing, and deployment of all nuclear weapons. This freeze was originally construed by its proponents as unilateral, for the United States only, but in view of the American public's sound instinctive insistence on Soviet reciprocity, it is now usually expressed as a bilateral U.S.-Soviet obligation to be achieved by mutual agreement.

Yet whether the intended objective is a unilateral or a bilateral freeze, the freeze proposal in its actual effect is as counterproductive and diversionary as would be a physician's promise to a cancer patient that he can "freeze" the cancer, presumably rendering it ineffective, even though such a promise does not actually diminish the threat posed by the existing disease. In reality, nuclear weapons would not be "frozen" into ineffectiveness even if, as is extremely unlikely, a bilateral freeze on all types of nuclear weapons could be effectively verified. They would, in fact, remain fully operational, or "hot." Their numbers would not diminish, and arms-reduction negotiations would be seriously undercut. The high numbers of arms would be legitimized by a freeze.

In short, a declaration of good intent is not enough as an objective, no matter what the problem. The ethical imperative and professional task, I believe, is to analyze the nature of the problem and its causes and to reduce its effect certifiably, with the aim of actually controlling and eventually eliminating it. In this process, the physician, or by analogy the statesman, should learn from previous efforts to control the disease. He should especially note whether any of those prior efforts involved placebos or illusions that actually accelerated the growth of the disease instead of reducing or eliminating its causes and its effects.

In addition to avoiding illusory remedies, I believe the physician or statesman should also seek to take full advantage of new technologies and new ways of thinking about the problem, as does President Reagan's Strategic Defense Initiative of March 23, 1983. This initiative proposes intensive long-term research into the feasibility of securing greater global stability and safety by emphasizing deterrence through defensive rather than offensive systems. The initiative seeks to shift from the current reliance of nuclear deterrence exclusively on offensive forces that can annihilate an adversary and destroy much of the world, to a new approach that integrates strategic defense, particularly non-nuclear systems, into strategic deterrence and thereby substantially reduces the incentives for deploying offensive nuclear weapons, or threatening their use.

ARMS-CONTROL POLICY OF THE REAGAN ADMINISTRATION

When President Reagan was still a candidate for the presidency, he and his bipartisan group of senior advisors articulated a philosophy of arms control that his administration has pursued with consistency and on an ethical basis. I have worked in the U.S. government for five presidents, for four of these as a member of the National Security Council staff, and I believe that the Reagan administration's nuclear arms-control policies and negotiating proposals involve objectives and criteria that are far sounder, far bolder, and more worthy of support, ethically and diplomatically, than those of his predecessors.

1. Reductions

The first of these criteria is that *arms-control negotiations must be directed toward substantially reducing and effectively constraining arms*. In previous administrations, regrettably, negotiations too often aimed only at codifying very high numbers or "ceilings" for existing arsenals as the best we could seek to achieve. Or earlier negotiations sought merely to slow, but not dramatically to reverse, the rate of growth. Or limits on the development of new capabilities were agreed that then proved ambiguous, largely unverifiable, and unenforceable and thus tolerated enormous arms increases within the framework of arms-control agreements.

In sharp contrast, President Reagan has proposed deep arms *reductions* as a principal criterion of real arms control. The reductions and related constraints proposed by the Reagan administration are very substantial, not merely cosmetic. And they seek to reduce both current arsenals and future capabilities.

2. Equal Levels

A second criterion is that *arms reductions must lead to equal levels for both sides*. The concept of equal levels takes into account not only numbers but also capabilities. In essence, this criterion corresponds to the legislative mandate set forth in the so-called Jackson Amendment to the SALT I agreement—the Interim Agreement on offensive weapons as ratified by the United States Senate in 1972. This amendment states that, as of 1972, all future negotiations by the United States with respect to strategic nuclear weapons should be on the basis of equal U.S. and Soviet levels. The Jackson Amendment represents an authentic congressional mandate since it was part of the treaty-ratification package passed by a vote of eighty-eight to two. SALT I could not have achieved ratification without this amendment.

This important amendment related directly to the growing interest in the concept of equal capabilities as a measure of enhancing strategic stability through arms control. Members of Congress were concerned that SALT I had set unequal levels for the two parties. SALT I permitted the Soviet Union to develop strategic forces numbering about one-third more launchers than the American forces, with the potential for even greater disparities in significant measures of strategic capability. The U.S. negotiators allowed this disparity because they apparently believed that, to have parity in overall capability, we should allow the Soviet Union to have more weapons, since it was thought to have inferior technology. Unfortunately, this generous approach quickly proved destabilizing for arms control in the face of the unexpectedly rapid improvement of Soviet weapons. This improvement was, ironically, in significant measure attributable to the Soviet Union's acquisition of advanced Western technology by theft or by commercial transfer.

When these very substantial technological improvements occurred in Soviet operational systems after 1972, the result was that, not only did the Soviet Union now have the superior number of strategic forces allocated to it by the SALT I treaty, but its weapons systems had become very comparable to the American systems in quality. Its higher numbers of such high-quality systems provided the Soviet Union major advantages destabilizing to the strategic balance. In particular, as spelled out below, the Soviet Union had by the late 1970s achieved a first-strike capability against the United States.

Although such a dangerous imbalance apparently was not anticipated by the SALT I negotiators, a concerned Senate in 1972 through the Jackson Amendment sought to assure a more balanced stance for all future negotiations, a position to be based on an equality that takes into account not only numbers but also capabilities and changed conditions. The Reagan administration supports this congressional concept of overall equality as being very much in the best interests of arms control, of U.S. security, and of global stability, and has consistently sought to implement it in its arms-control negotiations.

3. Effective Verification

The administration's third fundamental criterion of responsible negotiations for arms control is that *any agreements reached must be effectively verifiable*. National security requires that the United States ensure it can monitor compliance with agreements. Monitoring has depended largely upon satellites and other national technical means possessed by the United States and the Soviet Union. At one time inferior Soviet capability, coupled with American mastery in such areas as outer space and electronics, allowed us to depend exclusively upon verification procedures that did not require on-site monitoring and inspection and that were able to discover essentially all important activities. But today's increasingly capable Soviet military industry, new mobile systems, and the massive Soviet use of encryption, deception, and camouflage make such remote verification more difficult and the likelihood of Soviet cheating much greater.

The realities of the Soviet Union's improved technology, expanded military capability, and great secrecy mean that effective verification will require better technology and also means of monitoring agreements that go beyond the remote technical methods considered sufficient in the past to include a variety of confidence-building and cooperative measures, including on-site inspections. Naturally, whatever verification methods are necessary to assure compliance will be applied equally to the United States and the Soviet Union.

I believe that these three criteria form a sound basis for the Reagan administration's approach to arms control. Other important factors helping to shape the arms-control policy of the United States include historical, geopolitical, and military developments and lessons of the last decade.

HISTORICAL AND GEOPOLITICAL CONTEXT

Arms-control efforts, including a given administration's understanding and efforts, do not occur as on a *tabula rasa* but are profoundly affected by historical experience. The experience of reaching major arms-control agreements with the Soviet Union in 1972—the SALT I agreements on limiting offensive systems and on limiting anti-ballistic-missile systems—initially caused the American government and people to have great optimism about future progress. Reinforcing this optimism was the widespread belief that the negotiations and summit meetings of the time had fundamentally altered the international atmosphere, particularly in regard to the superpowers' view of a common interest. In 1972 there was widespread hope that the SALT I agreements signed in Moscow that year would be implemented both in letter and in spirit. Later, as events increasingly contradicted these hopes, evidence of violations of the "détente" spirit that had provided a diplomatic context for the arms-control agreements at that time was generally ignored or dismissed. Arms-control efforts suffered from major illusions and setbacks, and it is important to understand this record.

At the June 1972 summit meeting in Moscow, the superpowers not only formally signed the arms-control agreements but also formally pledged to engage in "détente" and to practice "peaceful coexistence." Moscow and Washington pledged that they would not take unilateral advantage of each other, that they would settle disputes peacefully, and that they would avoid confrontation. It was expected, in the optimistic atmosphere of the time, that the results of "détente" would permit reduced defense spending, enabling both nations to concentrate more on domestic development and reform. But the chapters of history written in the 1970s and early eighties were to demonstrate that under "détente" one of the two superpowers actually undertook something quite different.

Early Violations of Détente

Let me give some historical examples. In the fall of 1973, within a year of the SALT I agreements and the peaceful-coexistence pledges of 1972, several Arab states, with Soviet knowledge and support, renewed hostilities against Israel in a surprise attack. At the same time, the Soviets marshalled their own military forces (including readying seven airborne divisions), deployed a large armada in the eastern Mediterranean, and initiated a massive resupply effort, which necessitated an American effort to reinforce the Israelis. A cease-fire agreement was finally reached via American diplomacy, but the Soviet Union was of essentially no help at all in the negotiations and contributed to tensions rather than reducing them.

A second example: In January 1973 the Soviet Union became a co-guarantor of the armistice agreement signed on Vietnam, as a result of which the few remaining American combat forces were withdrawn from that tragic conflict. But the armistice was crudely broken within two years, when early in 1975 many new North Vietnamese divisions stormed into South Vietnam, soon overrunning all of Laos and eastern Cambodia as well. These new divisions augmented the numerous North Vietnamese forces already fighting in those states. The fighting that resulted from this massive invasion wrecked the armistice agreement, destroyed South Vietnam's hopes for freedom, precipitated a terrible genocidal massacre in Cambodia, and ended a local balance of power in Laos. Today more than 100,000 North Vietnamese troops still subjugate Laos, while more than 250,000 others fight for control of Cambodia.

In all this, the Soviets, though guarantors of the violated armistice agreement, did nothing to encourage restraint by the North Vietnamese. They showed little concern for the persons, governments, and institutions that their allies, using Soviet weapons, victimized, and in the process they showed their lack of respect for the principles of peaceful coexistence. While the human rights of millions of Southeast Asians have been systematically violated by regimes loyal to the Soviet Union and dependent on Soviet assistance, Moscow has not seen fit to exercise either moral or diplomatic responsibility in the matter. In the areas occupied by the North Vietnamese divisions, there is neither peace nor freedom, and religious persecution looms large. Almost all Buddhist and Christian leadership of the overrun countries has disappeared; believers have been subject to persecution, forcible expulsion, imprisonment, and death. Vietnam's Cam Ranh Bay is now a major Soviet military base.

In the 1970s and beyond, Africa also did not escape the Soviets' perversion of what they called "détente" or "peaceful coexistence." Cuba, like North Vietnam a militant and expansionist Soviet client, in 1975 sent some 20,000 troops across the Atlantic Ocean to Angola at the request of a Marxist revolutionary movement that in the wake of Portuguese withdrawal was struggling for power with two other political movements. That same Soviet client, Cuba, sent some 20,000 other troops thousands of miles away to eastern Africa to join Soviet military commanders and East German instructors in Ethiopia in 1976-77. These Cuban forces assure internal security and support two Ethiopian wars, one against neighboring Somalia and the other against a revolutionary movement in the dissident area of Eritrea. Such extraordinary Soviet actions would be the equivalent, in terms of abusing "détente," of the United States' sending, or persuading some ally to send, 40,000 troops into months and years of combat inside African nations. Such Soviet/Cuban behavior could not fail to have a detrimental impact upon the relationship between the superpowers, including the trust required to achieve real progress in reducing the levels of arms.

Later Violations of Détente

More recently, other Soviet actions in the Middle East, Europe, and Central America further eroded both the spirit and the letter of "détente." First, when Iranian revolutionaries seized the United States Embassy and hundreds of U.S. diplomats in Teheran in November 1979 in the wake of uprisings to protest the deposed Shah's presence in the United States, the action had been preceded by Radio Moscow broadcasts in the Farsi language encouraging the militants to take such a step.

Second, in December 1979, the Soviets invaded Afghanistan, a move involving some 100,000 troops and their equipment, including armored divisions, heavy artillery, and aircraft. This Soviet move was precipitated when the Afghan government previously supported by the Soviets sought greater independence from Moscow. The leaders of that regime were murdered as Soviet troops flew into the capital. So far the Soviet Union has refused to withdraw its divisions or submit the dispute to negotiation. And to the horror of the world the Soviets followed their original violation of Afghan sovereignty with the extensive use of outlawed lethal chemical weapons.

Third, in Poland, Soviet reaction to the population's desire for reform has been repression, at times accompanied by blunt military pressure.

Fourth, the Western Hemisphere has felt the direct force of Soviet activity as militant revolutionary movements in several Central American states have fallen under Soviet or Cuban manipulation or control. Events in Nicaragua and El Salvador, and the Soviet efforts to establish a major military and revolutionary base in Grenada, have provided much direct evidence of the extent to which the Soviet Union and its militant surrogates abused the era the world expected to be one of true "détente." Far from upholding the principle of peaceful coexistence, the Soviet Union engaged in subverting legitimate human aspirations and undermining governments that resist reactionary Soviet imperial authority while buttressing those that are Moscow's pawns. This history necessarily had a sobering effect upon efforts to achieve agreements assuring genuine arms control and compelled insistence on the types of arms-control criteria advocated by the Reagan administration.

MILITARY DEVELOPMENTS

Certain military realities that form part of the present international context of arms-control efforts are at least as important and disturbing as the geopolitical ones illustrated above. The harsh truth is that while the United States, particularly during the past decade, acted with great restraint in its military programs, the Soviet Union did not. Let me give some examples.

Since I entered government service during the Kennedy administration, the proportion of the U.S. federal budget allocated to defense has declined from approximately one-half to about one-fourth. That is astonishing, and yet it is not generally known. Until quite recently, when inflation is taken into account, there was for years a real decline in defense spending. The "guns-to-butter" ratio in the U.S. budget reversed in favor of "butter"—i.e., social expenditures—during the first Nixon administration and has remained reversed, although the rapid increase in social spending has recently leveled off. (See chart 1, page 45.)

Yet at the same time that the U.S. defense budget began its decade of relative decline, a process that accelerated after the military wind-down and final U.S. withdrawal from Vietnam, the Soviet Union's military budget continued the dramatic climb that had begun even before the SALT I negotiations concluded until, with half of our gross national product, they began to outspend us substantially at about the same time our guns and butter lines crossed. (See chart 2.) While the Soviets reveal virtually nothing about their national budget, the best U.S. estimates indicated that Soviet defense spending in the 1970s was climbing by 3-4 per cent a year. This occurred despite a Soviet GNP that is under considerable strain.

The Soviet military budget is primarily devoted to the development and acquisition of weapons systems, including nuclear-capable systems and their combat support hardware. Relatively little is allocated to personnel costs or auxiliary services, for which well over half the U.S. defense budget is spent. The United States now spends about 6 per cent of its GNP on defense, while the Soviets spend more than twice that level. In the area of strategic nuclear weapons they have regularly outspent us by a factor of about three to one. Interestingly, only about 4 per cent of our national budget, or 12-14 per cent of our defense budget, is dedicated to strategic nuclear forces. (See chart 3, page 46.)

Reductions in the U.S. Arsenal

Even as the United States was reducing the size of its defense budget in relative terms during the seventies, it was doing something else very noteworthy: greatly reducing the actual number and the power of nuclear weapons in its possession. (See chart 4.) By 1982 the United States had reduced its nuclear arsenal by over 25 per cent below the level attained during the Johnson administration in the mid-sixties. Thus the United States has only three-quarters as many nuclear weapons as it once had.

But the reductions did not stop there, for the United States has also reduced the power of its nuclear arsenal by progressively reducing the yield of its warhead capacity. Between the mid-sixties and 1982, total U.S. megatonnage, an important measure of strategic nuclear firepower, shrank by 75 per cent. This means that by the early eighties the United States had 75 per cent *less* megatonnage, incorporated in 25 per cent *fewer* weapons, and operated on a relatively *smaller* defense budget, than a decade or so earlier.

The relative decline in the U.S. defense budget was reflected in a significant curtailment in the deployment of new strategic systems. The 1960s saw the last deployment of new U.S. strategic weapons systems until the end of the 1970s. Even systems presently being developed or soon to be deployed, such as the new Trident class submarine and the future MX missile and B-1 bomber, involve programs initiated during the sixties but then delayed or canceled during the "détente" of the seventies. After the SALT I treaty was signed in 1972, the United States virtually suspended the deployment of new strategic weapons systems, and also markedly slowed down its research and development efforts. But not so the Soviet Union, which embarked on the greatest arms buildup in history.

The Strategic Imbalance

As the following examples demonstrate, the situation regarding deployed strategic systems became very unbalanced by the late 1970s.

The United States in the fall of 1983 had one new Trident submarine deployed, with one undergoing sea trials and another nearing deployment. This represented the total new deployment of American strategic ballistic-missile submarines for a twenty-year period since the early 1960s, when our last Poseidon was deployed. In contrast, during the seventies alone the Soviet Union deployed more than sixty new ballistic-missile submarines in five new classes, including the Yankee, the Delta I, Delta II, and Delta III, and the world's largest class, the Typhoon. While the United States still leads in the number of submarine-based missile *warheads*, the Soviets have more *submarines* and more *missiles* and are adding more of both at a fast pace. The United States in the fall of 1983 had 568 missiles in 34 submarines, a figure that will decline as old vessels are retired, while the Soviets had more than 950 larger missiles in 62 submarines. The Soviet submarine fleet is, on the average, nearly a decade younger than the U.S. fleet. In sum, between the 1972 SALT I accord and late 1983, the Soviets built more than sixty new strategic ballistic-missile submarines compared to our one or two new Tridents.

In the air the imbalance is even greater. The United States has deployed no new strategic bomber since 1962. Since that was the latest date at which our newest B-52 bombers were built, many of these American bombers are older than the crew members who fly them. Meanwhile the Soviets have introduced well over two hundred intercontinental-range Backfire bombers, are getting ready to introduce the new Blackjack, and are also working on a more advanced bomber. Soviet intercontinental-range aircraft in service now substantially outnumber those in the active U.S. inventory. Meanwhile, deployment of the first new American bomber in two and a half decades, the B-1, will not begin until late 1986.

In intercontinental-range land-based missile forces (ICBMs), the Soviets since SALT I in 1972 have added 800 new ICBMs with thousands of warheads, the United States zero new missiles. During the last decade or so the Soviets introduced at least three very modern ICBM types, the SS-17, SS-18, and SS-19, and they may also have deployed some SS-16s. In contrast, the last new American ICBM was the Minuteman III, deployed in 1969. Furthermore, the United States has had a decreasing number of land-based missiles since 1965, when we began retiring our oldest ICBMs, and we are now systematically retiring all the remaining Titan missiles.

These sharply contrasting military trends must be taken into account in any serious effort for effective arms control. In the mid-sixties Defense Secretary Robert McNamara argued that the United States was so far ahead of the Soviets that the Soviets should be allowed to achieve parity. McNamara's assumption was that once parity was reached the Soviets would negotiate a good-faith agreement to halt further increases. He was wrong. In 1965 the United States had approximately 1,000 ICBMs to the Soviets' 200-250. But the United States stayed at 1,000 and the Soviets continued to deploy more and larger missiles. By 1972 there was approximate overall parity, counting land-, sea-, and air-based systems, as the SALT I negotiations acknowledged. Then the Soviets forged ahead, espcially in ICBMs. They continued to build and to deploy and to test, and they are still doing so.

Today the Soviets have about 1,400 ICBMs with more than 6,000 warheads. The most modern Soviet ICBM, the SS-18, has ten warheads, each of them more powerful than the total power of all three warheads on a U.S. Minuteman III. That makes each of these newer Soviet ICBMs thirty times more destructive than the most modern U.S. ICBMs. Down the road, two more classes of Soviet ICBMs are currently being tested for deployment (at least one in violation of Soviet arms-control commitments). The new American ICBM, the MX, has yet to complete testing and will not be deployed until late 1986. (It is also relevant to note that newer intermediate-range Soviet missiles, such as more than 360 triple-warhead SS-20s, were deployed in the six years preceding the fall of 1983, while the United States had deployed no comparable missiles—a ratio in deployed intermediate-range missile warheads of more than 1,000 for the Soviet Union to zero for the United States.)

The SALT II Treaty

Some of the new Soviet ICBMs were already deployed when President Carter presented the SALT II treaty to the Senate in 1979.

When his administration was asked what it intended to do about the large new Soviet missiles, the SS-18s, which some senators regarded as particularly destabilizing, the response was that the treaty would "freeze" the numbers of heavy missiles on both sides. However, a freeze on heavy missiles meant that the United States, which had no such missiles, would have no right to any, thus remaining at zero, while the Soviet Union would legitimately keep the more than 300 SS-18 missiles with over 3,000 warheads it had already deployed. And as for limiting the buildup in other missiles and warheads, the *rate of buildup* might be slowed under SALT II, but the buildup itself would continue to higher levels and there would be no reductions in warheads.

This ICBM inequality was one of the profound problems with the proposed SALT II agreement that led the U.S. Senate, including many members considered "doves," to criticize it severely. I believe Senator McGovern was one who indicated at the time that he would not vote for what he and others characterized as not a document of arms *control* but one legitimizing arms *escalation*. In addition to the missile problem, the proposed SALT II agreement legitimized the production of thirty Backfire bombers a year; it contained a protocol, highly objectionable to our allies, on restricting cruise missiles; and much of the provision for verification was quite unsatisfactory, especially after the loss of important American intelligence-gathering sites in Iran. As to the number of multiple-warhead strategic missiles, SALT II allowed about a one-third *increase* in the U.S. force and about a *doubling* of the newer Soviet force.

Far from being a sound instrument of nuclear arms reductions, the proposed SALT II treaty legitimized an enormous arms buildup and destabilizing new imbalances. It was opposed by the Senate Armed Services Committee as unequal, unverifiable, and against the U.S. national security interest. It was headed for numerous major amendments or outright congressional defeat. Governor Reagan and his advisors considered it fatally flawed. Finally, with radical changes or certain defeat imminent, President Carter withdrew the proposed treaty from consideration by the Democratic-controlled Senate following the Soviet invasion of Afghanistan in December 1979.

Another way of looking at the strategic arms situation is to note that by the late seventies the Soviets had deployed at least three strategic ICBM warheads, able to destroy even concrete hardened targets rapidly, for every single U.S. missile silo (land-based U.S. missiles, like the Soviet ICBMs, are housed in hardened underground silos). (See chart 5.) It is generally thought by specialists that at least two modern ICBM warheads are required to ensure destruction of a single hardened target, such as a missile silo or a command bunker. Once a potential attacker's ratio goes over two or three such warheads per target, he is considered to have first-strike capability, at least theoretically. This means that he may perceive the certainty of destruction as large enough that if he were to launch a strike he could eliminate all, or almost all, of his opponent's missiles and hardened command systems.

The United States has not wanted a first-strike capability, and we do not possess one. The U.S. possesses approximately 1,000 ICBMs (the land-based missiles), with some 2,200 warheads. There are about 1,400 known Soviet strategic missile silos and numerous hardened Soviet command bunkers. This means that the United States has only about 1½-to-1 ratio of warheads to Soviet missile silos, and an even lower ratio when the numerous Soviet command bunkers are considered. Unlike the Soviet Union, the United States has clearly not sought a first-strike capability. At the same time, in the face of the Soviet first-strike threat, the United States has not adopted policies such as "launch-on-warning" that have been proposed by some non-government critics of the Administration as a deterrent against a Soviet first strike. The Administration considers a launch-on-warning policy to be destabilizing and highly dangerous. I believe the adoption of such a destabilizing policy would also raise particularly difficult ethical questions.

It must be added that submarine-based missile warheads, in which the United States has held a numerical lead over the Soviet Union, do not have the accuracy or yield to destroy hardened missile silos or bunkers. With current technology they can be used only against non-hardened sites and are not first-strike weapons. But by the late 1980s submarine missile technology *will* enable the warheads to destroy some hardened military targets, a fact that should increase the Soviet and U.S. incentive to reach bilateral arms-reduction agreements before that time.

THE START NEGOTIATIONS

In the Strategic Arms Reduction Talks (START), which the Reagan administration began with the Soviet Union in Geneva in mid-1982, the United States tried at the outset to distinguish between the more destabilizing and vulnerable first-strike land-based weapons, described above, on the one hand, and submarine-launched weapons on the other, and to emphasize reductions in the former. The U.S. negotiating stance recognized, however, that the Soviets had some 75 per cent of their missiles based on land and did not wish to make such a distinction, which they considered as imposing a major restructuring of their forces.

In light of this Soviet view, the United States subsequently proposed that the present number of *all* strategic ballistic missiles, whether land-based or sea-based, be reduced to an equal level of 850 missiles on each side but with "freedom to mix" land- and sea-based missiles within that ceiling. The 850 ceiling represented a cut of nearly 50 per cent from the current U.S. level of 1,650 such missiles and even more of a reduction in the 2,200 Soviet missiles, though we subsequently indicated that we were prepared to be flexible about the 850 level. As a start on the road to reduction, the United States also proposed to reduce the number of warheads on strategic ballistic missiles, both land-based and sea-based, to 5,000 for each country, a cut of about one-third below existing U.S. and Soviet levels.

In sum, we would like to move to deep mutual cuts, and as a start we proposed a one-third cut in warheads carried and a reduction by one-half in the number of missiles below existing U.S. levels. We also seek to reduce bomber numbers and the throwweight of the ballistic missiles. (See chart 6, page 49.)

Moscow's Negative Response

Soviet responses to these dramatic U.S. START proposals of 1982 and 1983 were negative and concentrated on the fact that the Soviet Union would have to eliminate more warheads and missiles than would the United States. The U.S. response was that this was true only because the Soviet Union had *produced and deployed* far more strategic missiles than we had; that, furthermore, our proposal is for deep reductions to *equal* U.S. and Soviet levels; and that the principle of equality must be honored at these lower levels if arms control is to be meaningful.

Another Soviet reaction was to declare that the proposed new levels would be too low, an objection also raised by some American critics. Ironically, some members of the U.S. arms-control community in the private sector appeared to think it outrageous and even unethical that President Reagan, whom many unjustly accused of not being serious about arms control, would propose such *deep* reductions. Their apparent reason for objecting to the low levels was that, since the Soviets objected, the bold U.S. proposals would make negotiations more difficult. Thus the Reagan administration was in the odd situation of being asked by some supposed proponents of arms control to seek far *less* dramatic arms reductions and to get back to the old cosmetic remedy of accepting major increases and high end numbers for the sake of agreement—any agreement.

Despite the Administration's determination to achieve significant reductions, and in recognition that the Soviets were not eager for major reductions, the United States during 1983 demonstrated significant new flexibility in its specific proposals. The central change was to suggest alternative paths to reductions. The United States is ready to consider various trade-offs in advantages on land, sea, and air. And we proposed a mutual "build-down," a term that emerged from ongoing bipartisan efforts to recommend arms-control policies having wide political support. The build-down concept grew out of consultations with senators and representatives from both parties. It had the support of the Scowcroft Commission, a high-level bipartisan commission appointed by the President to review specific security proposals. Under our build-down proposal, as alternatives to immediate large reductions, we would agree to annual 5 per cent reductions in all strategic systems and a set of ratios and trade-offs by which any newly introduced weapon would lead to the withdrawal of existing weapons in a proportion, for example, of three withdrawn for every two deployed.

The Administration believes that negotiating substantial strategic arms *reductions*, not diverting to negotiation of a "freeze," is in the true interests of arms control, and that negotiations on numbers, counting rules, and verification procedures of a freeze would be very involved and would directly undercut efforts and incentives for negotiations on arms reductions. The Soviet Union has already made counterproposals for a 25 per cent reduction in strategic weapons systems below the current levels, levels that had been accepted in the SALT II agreements, though the Soviets are weak on such matters as identifying specific systems and verification procedures. If we froze at current levels or ratified the SALT II treaty levels today, we would be retrogressing, legitimizing high arms levels and profoundly flawed arms-control concepts while essentially ending incentives for future reductions. The ethics of such a step would, I believe, be profoundly disturbing.

Old and New Strategic Systems

A major problem in strategic arms negotiations, and certainly another fundamental objection to any freeze proposal, involves the disparate ages of the strategic forces of the two superpowers. The great bulk of the Soviet strategic forces is less than five or six years old. This includes most of the new multiple-warhead ICBMs, the Backfire bomber, and the Typhoon class submarine. The only new U.S. strategic system fully operational as of late 1983 that was less than five years old was the one Trident missile submarine, the *Ohio*, with others being added slowly. The design of our Minuteman III ICBM system dates from before 1969, when the missile was deployed. Only the warhead deployed on two-thirds of the Minuteman III missiles is less than fifteen years old. The U.S. strategic ballistic-missile submarine fleet, except for the new Tridents, is over fifteen years old; most of it is past twenty. Our bomber force is between twenty and twenty-five years old. Such age has exacerbated strategic imbalances and makes U.S. modernization vital both to assure an effective deterrent and as an incentive for the Soviet Union to negotiate arms reductions.

Therefore the Administration is, with bipartisan congressional support, pressing ahead both with arms-reduction proposals and with modernization programs. This is no contradiction. The record shows that the Soviets do not come to the arms negotiating table and do not bargain seriously unless there are military programs under way in the United States. A classic example of this reality is the Anti-Ballistic-Missile Treaty of 1972. In the late 1960s the United States attempted to engage the Soviet Union in negotiations on anti-ballistic-missile (ABM) defense systems, but the Soviets refused. Then, within a few weeks of the one-vote margin by which the U.S. Senate in 1969 funded an ABM development program, the Soviets decided to negotiate. A very short time later the ABM treaty was completed, signed, and ratified.

One should note that the current strategic modernization programs being undertaken by the United States in response to years of Soviet buildup serve to promote serious negotiations as well as to make up for serious imbalances. Our strategic-arms negotiating stance, as previously stated, intends that such modernization neither be destabilizing nor contribute to *net* arms increases. It accomplishes these objectives by proposing the withdrawal of existing systems as new ones are introduced in such ratios that the strategic forces actually *decrease* to the proposed equal levels set forth in our reductions proposals.

THE INF NEGOTIATIONS

Of especially great concern to our European allies are the Intermediate-range Nuclear Forces (INF) negotiations. The main Soviet weapon in the INF category, the triple-warhead SS-20 mobile missile, has a range that can reach all of Europe, all of North Africa, the Middle East, and China with all three warheads mounted. It can reach into Alaska, and it is believed that with only two warheads mounted on it the SS-20 could easily reach all of Canada and the northern United States. With only one warhead mounted, all of the United States and the northern Caribbean region would be vulnerable. (See chart 7, page 50.)

As now deployed, the Soviet SS-20 has a range of 4,500 to 5,000 kilometers (approximately 3,000 miles). Each of its warheads is roughly equivalent to one of the U.S. Minuteman ICBM warheads. The SS-20 system is very closely related to the Soviets' SS-16 ICBM, a system that was to have been banned under SALT II. The SS-20 was developed in the mid-1960s, with the first deployment in 1977. Since that time the Soviets have deployed SS-20s at the rate of about one new missile with three warheads per week (in addition to their some 600 existing SS-4 and SS-5 INF missiles), despite the absence of any comparable new U.S. systems until late 1983. And while the Soviets have sometimes talked about a possible moratorium on SS-20 deployment, they have certainly not practiced one.

The range of the SS-20 enables it to reach Western Europe from launch sites east of the Ural Mountains—outside Europe. It is mobile and extremely well camouflaged; it can easily be transported; and its launcher can be reused. By the fall of 1983 there were more than 360 SS-20 launchers and missiles, making a total of nearly 1,100 warheads, plus at least one reload missile for each SS-20 launcher. It is inconceivable that the Soviet forces need to program more than 1,000 new European or Asian or Mideastern targets with their new SS-20s. They have more than enough coverage with their other missiles and with their aircraft. So why did they unilaterally deploy them? The United States had withdrawn its last intermediate-range missiles in the 1960s and for years had no missiles stationed in Europe capable of reaching Soviet territory.

The NATO Response

For three years, 1977-79, NATO's policy toward the growing SS-20 threat was to state that the new Soviet missiles (like the new Backfire bombers) were destabilizing, and to protest their deployment, while rejecting countermeasures of its own. In December 1979, after realizing the futility of protest, NATO at the request of its European members decided to pursue new rounds of U.S.-Soviet arms-control negotiations but, if that failed to achieve results, to deploy a limited number of intermediate-range missiles as a response. This deployment was seen as an effort to restore a measure of balance and increased deterrence in the face of the enormous Warsaw Pact buildup, and also as an incentive to the proposed INF arms-control negotiations.

The countersystems that NATO decided to deploy beginning in late 1983 were the American Pershing II and the Ground-Launched Cruise Missile (GLCM). The former is a small, mobile, single-warhead missile with high accuracy, but with a range less than half that of the SS-20. It could penetrate only a few hundred miles into Soviet territory from Western Europe and could not reach Moscow.

NATO also decided to supplement the very small number of 108 Pershing IIs with 464 GLCMs, small single-warhead jet-powered cruise missiles of longer range but slow speed. The total number of missiles in both these systems, to be deployed in the absence of an arms-control agreement, was to be 572, all with a single warhead. That totals 572 warheads, which is about half the number of Soviet SS-20 warheads deployed as of the fall of 1983 and less than half the total Soviet INF missile force if the SS-4 and SS-5 INF missiles are included.

To deal with this situation, the Reagan administration at the outset of the INF negotiations, which began in Geneva in November 1981, proposed to *eliminate* all such Soviet and U.S. systems— i.e., zero on both sides.

In view of these facts, why do the Soviet leaders, who have continued to deploy large numbers of the destabilizing SS-20 missiles since 1977, now accuse the West of upsetting the missile balance in Europe? Given the fact that the deployment of NATO's response is to be very gradual over several years beginning late in 1983, one views with incredulity the Soviet claim that it is NATO that is guilty of arms escalation and of undercutting the basis for INF arms negotiations. The Soviet-to-U.S. intermediate-range missile warhead ratio in late 1983 of about 1,400 to 0 can hardly be considered *Western* escalation. This is particularly the case since the NATO action is strictly tied to serious efforts to negotiate arms reductions, and since the NATO proposal is for *zero* levels of such weapons on both sides—thus eliminating the need for any Pershing II or GLCM deployment if the Soviet SS-20, SS-4, and SS-5 INF missiles are eliminated.

The Need for Incentives

While the logic of the Soviets' protests against NATO policy is difficult to understand, their negative political and, I believe, ethical impact is easy to see. No one in the West really wants to deploy such weapons, or any others, if not absolutely necessary. But if the West were unilaterally to cancel the deployment in the absence of an effective arms-reduction agreement, the result would be to end rather than to promote the possibility of successful negotiations. The Soviets could hardly be interested in talking to people who declare their intention of deploying a relatively small number of less capable weapons as a means of assuring a deterrent and as an incentive to negotiation, and who then under Soviet pressure unilaterally eliminate that deterrent and incentive without achieving a reduction agreement.

We should remember that in the summer of 1979 then Premier Leonid Brezhnev came to West Germany and told the Germans most energetically that the then pending NATO decision to deploy countermeasures would end the possibility of negotiations. But the Allies held fast, the NATO dual-track decision was implemented, and within a few months the Soviets were back at the negotiating table. The Soviets often threaten. Mr. Khrushchev once threatened the world at the United Nations, banging his shoe at the podium and ordering the West to get out of West Berlin. If we are serious about arms-control efforts, if we truly want to achieve equitable and verifiable reductions enhancing stability, we in the West must resist such threats by maintaining our strength, continuing to offer negotiations only on a sound basis, and holding true to sound principles.

The INF negotiations in Geneva have had their ups and downs. We are not optimistic in any foolish way, but we are hopeful that the Soviets will come to recognize that it is in their interest as much as ours to negotiate reductions either to zero for comparable U.S. and Soviet systems, which is what we would prefer, or to some mutually agreeable intermediate number on the path to zero. Our side has proposed various numbers from 50 to 150, but each time the Soviets have said *nyet*.

We also were willing to discuss the 1982 "walk in the woods" proposal, in which the Soviet and U.S. chief negotiators jointly put forth a formula for reductions. But while the United States had problems with the proposed formula, it was Moscow's immediate outright rejection that killed it and closed this informal discussion channel. The main reasons for the Soviet rejection seem to have been that the proposal would have permitted, i.e., legitimized, some seventy-five American-controlled systems and that it would not have counted the British or French *strategic* deterrent forces that the Soviets have sought to count in the INF balance.

On this last point, it has been the consistent policy of the United States that the national nuclear deterrents of Great Britain and France, and of the People's Republic of China: (1) involve strategic, not intermediate-range, or INF, forces and therefore do not belong in any INF negotiations, and (2) are not controlled by the United States and therefore cannot legitimately be considered in bilateral negotiations between the United States and the Soviet Union. Furthermore, the leaders of the three sovereign powers in London, Paris, and Beijing have all clearly stated that they absolutely will not accept the United States as a negotiating proxy for them in regard to their strategic forces but will consider joining multilateral strategic arms-reduction efforts *if and when* the two superpowers have very substantially reduced their own enormous strategic arsenals.

The Soviets' 162 Proposal

During 1983 the Soviets publicly said they would settle for having "only" 162 of their INF missiles targeted on Europe, a figure that they claimed was equal to the total of British and French INF missile forces—forces we consider strategic, not INF. But this Soviet number not only confused *strategic* and *intermediate* forces; it also assumed that the United States would stay at zero, hardly a fair bargain, and it failed to limit the Soviets' mobile SS-20s based *east* of the Urals.

But there are also other problems about what the Soviets might have meant by the figure 162. For example, if they meant *land-based* systems, which is what the intermediate-range talks currently emphasize, then 162 is problematical. The sum of British and French land-based longer-range missile systems is eighteen, all French, and all strategic. And since these French strategic missiles have single warheads, the eighteen French missiles would, if somehow (though improperly) compared to the SS-20, be equivalent to only *six* Soviet SS-20s with three warheads each, not 162 three-warhead missiles with a total of 486 warheads.

On the other hand, if the Soviets were talking about *sea-based* deterrents as well, the number is still wrong, for the total of British and French submarine missile forces, all strategic, amounted to only 112 warheads at the time of the Soviet proposals. And the Soviets have completely failed to count the large number of *their own* submarine-based weapons targeted on Europe. As for *aircraft*, if these are to be counted, this category too involves a large dis-

crepancy in favor of the Soviet Union. Finally, the possibility that
the Soviet number might take *future* British and French strategic
developments into consideration is not a proper rejoinder either,
since we would then need to consider the huge growth we expect
in future *Soviet* strategic deployments. It should be noted in this
connection that a decade ago British and French nuclear forces
were equal to some 9 per cent of Soviet nuclear forces but that in
view of the enormous Soviet buildup, they today equal only some
4 per cent of Soviet forces.

At any rate, the statements by both European powers and the
Chinese, that they are willing to consider entering the strategic talks
if and when the United States and the USSR achieve deep cuts
through their bilateral efforts, are considered by the Reagan administration to be both fair and constructive.

THE BROADER U.S. ARMS-CONTROL AGENDA

Present U.S. arms-control efforts with the Soviet Union cover a
wide variety of issues, and several of these efforts are multilateral
rather than bilateral. We have spoken thus far about the Strategic
Arms Reduction Talks (START) and the Intermediate-range Nuclear
Forces (INF) negotiations in Geneva. But the Administration's
arms-control agenda is far broader.

In Vienna, the United States and its allies are negotiating with
the USSR and other Warsaw Pact countries on the issues of Mutual
and Balanced Force Reductions (MBFR), embracing conventional
weapons systems. These negotiations emphasize reducing military
personnel strengths to lower and equal levels. In MBFR, the United
States and its NATO allies have made wide-ranging proposals; for
instance, in 1982 they proposed new confidence-building measures
such as information exchanges, observers, and new verification
procedures. [Note: In April 1984 the United States and its allies
made a new MBFR proposal, which like the 1982 proposal was
rejected by the Soviet Union.]

Another set of Geneva-based arms-control efforts involves the
Committee on Disarmament, where the United States and thirty-
nine other states are working on diverse arms-control efforts including an effectively verifiable ban on the manufacture, storage, and

transfer of chemical weapons. The Geneva Protocols of 1925 already ban their use, but that is a ban that the Soviets and their allies have systematically violated in Cambodia, Laos, and Afghanistan. Because of the huge Soviet chemical-warfare program, the United States has reluctantly proposed to modernize its own chemical arsenal and defenses in order to have a convincing deterrent and as an incentive to negotiations, but we have said we are quite prepared to eliminate all of our chemical capability if a verifiable ban can be reached.

The Need for Better Verification and Compliance

Other arms-control efforts in which the United States is engaged with the Soviet Union involve the search for improved verification procedures for nuclear test limitations and for possible arms control in outer space. Existing nuclear test-limitation agreements have apparently not prevented Soviet tests exceeding the 150-kiloton limit. Furthermore, they are difficult to verify accurately, and they give the Soviets escape clauses on the matter of on-site inspection; the local national authority can veto any such inspection. Verification of possible arms limitations in space, where the Soviets have since 1972 had the world's only operational anti-satellite system, also appears very difficult to achieve, but we are continuing to work hard on this problem.

Verification is a crucial issue in sound arms-control negotiations and agreements. It is of profound concern to us that the Soviet Union's record of sharing data and of complying with agreements is not good. The Soviets are very reluctant to provide information about their forces, even that which is minimally necessary to fulfill treaty obligations. They regard their military budgets and systems as very vital state secrets. They practice extensive data denial, camouflage, and deception. They have violated major arms-control agreements.

For our part, we are in compliance with agreements, and, in addition we believe it is important for countries increasingly to share information about their defense systems, especially when they are in a formal negotiation and when the information is vital to effective arms control and to international stability.

While no one is under the illusion that the totalitarian Soviet Union will turn into an open society tomorrow, the United States does believe that we and other nations must continue to try to persuade the Soviets to accept, for the sake of progress in arms control and for the building of trust, more effective information exchanges and verification measures than they now accept. Some progress has been made in various negotiations concerning confidence-building measures, including data exchanges to reduce the chances of accidents or misunderstandings. We will try to do more in this area in the future, as at the conference in Stockholm beginning in January 1984 on Security and Confidence Building in Europe, where we and our allies will be making specific proposals. [Note: In 1984 the United States and its Western allies proposed six specific confidence-building measures designed to build trust and to reduce the risks of war.]

CRITICS' ALTERNATIVES TO PRESENT NATO POLICY

In opposition to, and perhaps largely in ignorance of, the above ethical, technical, and diplomatic considerations, various individuals and groups of critics have put forth arms-control proposals radically different from those presented by the Administration. But some of the most prominent of these proposals contain fundamental flaws of analysis and application. They are largely counterproductive to the achievement of real reductions and real constraints and therefore do not deserve our considered support. Let me give a few examples.

1. A Freeze

Several groups are promoting the idea of a so-called freeze on nuclear arms. Such a freeze, as generally advocated in the United States, would be bilateral, not unilateral, thus requiring agreement, and would in theory halt all new nuclear arms production, testing, and deployment. Its proponents appear to see it as a helpful first step toward productive negotiations. Yet the difficulties and destabilizing implications of a freeze are severe, as we have seen in the previous discussion.

Consider, first, that there are major imbalances in age and numbers of strategic and intermediate-range nuclear forces, as well as in conventional systems. Freeze advocates are simply wrong when they say that the forces on both sides are roughly equal and that this balance should be codified. In fact, a freeze legitimizes the advantages achieved by the unparalleled Soviet buildup of the past ten to fifteen years.

Second, a bilateral freeze on production, testing, and deployment would require an *agreed* data base and *agreement* on very extensive, intrusive verification measures, which would in turn require very extensive negotiations, in direct conflict with any efforts to negotiate on arms *reductions*. Surely, to continue negotiations on arms reductions and stability at lower levels is a sounder and more urgent goal than undertaking arduous new negotiations about legitimizing the dangerous status quo.

Third, a freeze would push aside NATO's dual-track modernization/arms-control decision of 1979 concerning Intermediate-range Nuclear Forces (INF) without having achieved any Soviet INF reductions.

Fourth, history—including the history of arms-control negotiations—provides no evidence that the Soviets are inclined to negotiate seriously when they are ahead any more than when they are behind, unless incentives are provided in the form of Western programs. The West's willingness to modernize its strategic and INF systems in the face of the unprecedented Soviet military buildup is a very strong incentive for the Soviets to take seriously negotiations on reductions to equal levels.

In sum, a unilateral freeze would lock in Soviet advantages and be largely unverifiable, thus giving the Soviet Union clear military superiority and creating major new instabilities and risks. Moreover, the negotiation of a bilateral freeze, even if all its production, testing, and deployment provisions could indeed be made verifiable by the extensive on-site monitoring procedures required, would be a completely counterproductive diversion from negotiations on reductions. A freeze would codify the Soviet buildup and Soviet advantages and would eliminate any Soviet incentive to negotiate a reduction either in the number or in the deadliness of existing nuclear arsenals.

2. No First Use

Another frequently heard proposal is for adoption of a "no first use" policy by which the United States would pledge never to be the first to use nuclear weapons under any circumstances whatso-ever. This concept has been advanced by some prominent arms-control figures as well as by some religious organizations as a significant ethical and diplomatic contribution to arms control. To understand it, we must first distinguish between "no first use" and "no first strike," with which it is often confused.

A first strike—that is, launching nuclear weapons to destroy an opponent's nuclear arsenal in his home bases before that arsenal can be used—initiates an attack on the opponent and becomes possible if a nation possesses the means and the will for such an attack. As stated previously, such capability requires a ratio of at least two warheads to every hardened target such as missile silos or command bunkers, and at least one warhead for every non-hardened military target.

Clearly, there is only one possible source of a first-strike strategy in our world today, because there is only one power with such capability. The United States does not have it. The Soviet Union, however, now has first-strike capability in relation to American land-based missile silos, air bases, and naval bases. The only ele-ments of the U.S. nuclear arsenal that might escape a first strike by the Soviet Union are our missiles based on submarines at sea and those aircraft in our aging bomber fleet that manage to get airborne. But the submarine weapons cannot knock out hardened targets, and the bombers are slow flying and would encounter an extensive Soviet network of modern air defenses.

It has always been U.S. policy not to launch a first strike, and there is no debate about this policy commitment. The United States has no first-strike intention and, unlike the Soviet Union, has not sought and does not possess a first-strike capability. Meanwhile, however, the Soviet first-strike capability exists and must be taken into account by all who seek responsible arms control.

"No first use" of nuclear weapons is a separate concept from "no first strike." It does not refer to launching a first attack designed to destroy an enemy's arsenal. Instead, it would involve the political statement not to be the first to use nuclear weapons under *any* circumstances, including defense against aggression by non-nuclear forces.

The no-first-use concept was discussed by the U.S. Roman Cath-olic bishops in 1983, and an examination of their discussion is useful,

particularly since their actual position on this issue is often miscon-
strued.

The American bishops in their Pastoral Letter on War and Peace
propose that the United States government seek to develop a policy
of "no first use" of nuclear weapons. They do so on ethical grounds
common to many groups advocating a variety of similar positions,
namely, that the *use* of nuclear weapons is always immoral. Significantly, however, the bishops state the moral case *for* nuclear *deterrence* in a world of nuclear weapons, though with an important
caveat. They quote Pope John Paul II in saying that the *possession*
of nuclear weapons for the sake of deterring war can be considered
moral as long as such possession is seen as an intermediate step
paralleled by serious efforts toward disarmament. Thus *possession*
can still be viewed as moral while *use* is considered immoral.

The military and ethical dilemma that the bishops do not resolve
is that if a nation possesses nuclear weapons for deterrence, does
not this imply a credible willingness to use such weapons? And if
that is the case, then how can a meaningful distinction be sought
between the morality of possessing nuclear weapons and the immor-
ality of their possible use? This is an important question that deserves
further reflection.

But to return to what the bishops say about "no first use": I
believe the key to understanding the problem they put forth is in
the papal admonition that they affirm. Possession is moral as an
interim step on the way to disarmament, and thus nuclear weapons
arsenals may, in their opinion, exist ethically to deter war as long
as, but only as long as, serious arms-control negotiating efforts are
being made. It is noteworthy that the bishops in the final draft of
their pastoral letter recognize and support the extensive U.S.-Soviet
arms-reduction negotiations described above. This is an important
step, for they had failed to mention these negotiation efforts in the
earlier drafts of the letter.

The Conventional Imbalance

In requiring and supporting serious arms-control negotiation efforts,
the bishops do not abandon their call that the United States move
toward a policy of no first use of nuclear weapons. But they very
significantly circumscribe this call. The bishops clearly indicate

that, given the widely recognized preponderance of non-nuclear *conventional* military power in the hands of the Soviet Union and the Warsaw Pact, they do not support an immediate U.S. pledge of no first use of nuclear weapons. They understand that in the face of massive conventional attack, such a pledge would undermine deterrence and thus would be highly destabilizing. Instead, their pastoral letter advocates a conventional arms *buildup* on the part of the West to counterbalance Soviet conventional power, and the implementation of a no-first-use policy only *if* a balance of conventional forces can be developed.

I believe the bishops only gradually became aware that Soviet/ Warsaw Pact conventional weapons systems greatly outnumber their Western counterparts and that, therefore, a U.S. no-first-use declaration would be destabilizing. In tanks, armored personnel carriers, artillery, and other systems, the ratio is about two or three or more to one in favor of the Soviet forces. (See chart 8.) Similarly, U.S. and Western arms production has not come close to matching Soviet arms production. For example, the Reagan administration has sought to increase U.S. tank production from about 300 a year to perhaps 600-700 a year. This increase is small, however, in comparison to the Soviet production rate of 2,500-3,000 tanks a year over the past decade. Aircraft production and deployment is similarly unbalanced both between the USSR and the United States and between the Warsaw Pact and NATO.

While saying that Western conventional arms should first be built up to equal the Soviet/Warsaw Pact level, a stipulation made by other advocates of "no first use" as well, the bishops are nevertheless aware of severe Western political and economic limitations on this score. In their pastoral letter they appear aware that such a conventional force buildup is unlikely to occur because of the great *cost* of trying to match the huge and very modern Soviet and Warsaw Pact conventional forces. The bishops realize the substantial economic and political obstacles to increasing the level of NATO's conventional arms, though the NATO countries are seeking to use technology better to bridge the continuing numbers gap.

After thus examining the U.S. Catholic bishops' discussion of "no first use," what can one conclude about their bottom line on this issue? My own impression is that the bishops' view about what the U.S. government can and should do about adopting a no-first-use policy at this time is not really very different from the view of the U.S. government: neither the bishops nor the government believes it to be appropriate under current circumstances. The United States has consistently declared that it will never be the first to use *any* weapon in waging war, whether conventional or nuclear, and that its forces exist only to deter and to defend against attack within the Charter of the United Nations. American policy is that in case of an attack the United States will employ a policy of flexible response, which means that American forces will be used only in defense and only as minimally as possible to achieve stability and prevent greater violence while seeking political solutions through negotiations. The United States adheres to both United Nations and NATO obligations as well as to its own values and policy, all of which prohibit aggression while permitting individual and collective defense.

The Administration, like the U.S. Congress and like the Catholic bishops, is concerned about the conventional imbalance. We and our allies are making a serious long-term effort to modernize and improve the conventional forces of the West, even as we are substantially reducing by several thousand, or about a third, the nuclear weapon systems we have in Europe. The bishops are right to have no illusions about the chances for quickly or easily achieving a conventional balance, however, and the Administration shares that realism.

For this reason the United States agrees that immediate adoption of a no-first-use pledge would be unwise. Such a declaratory policy pledge on top of existing international commitments would be quite unverifiable and meaningless, a dangerous illusion, as long as one power possessed a strategic first-strike capability as well as overwhelming conventional force. It is far sounder to reduce arsenals and the risk of war through concrete arms-reduction and confidence-building measures as proposed by the United States in a number of nuclear and conventional force negotiations.

U.S. ARMS-CONTROL HOPES

Many arguments in favor of now adopting a no-first-use policy neglect what the U.S. Roman Catholic bishops have understood, which is that there is no balance of conventional weapons. Most such arguments also neglect the fact that nuclear weapons are not the only arms that are dangerous to human life or that involve severe ethical dilemmas. For example, lethal chemical and biological weapons, of which the Soviets have large inventories and which they or their allies have used in Afghanistan, Laos, and Cambodia, certainly fit this category, as do other types of non-nuclear weapons. Many persons alive today remember World Wars I and II and other wars, of which there have been more than 140 since the end of World War II. In President Reagan's lifetime the United States has been in four major wars. I myself experienced World War II directly in Germany as a British child held hostage by the German government for the duration of the war. All of us who witnessed such a war can attest to the extraordinary destructive power of even non-nuclear arms, as in the cities of Dresden, Warsaw, and Tokyo or on the battlefields of Europe, Asia, and Africa. With conviction born of experience, the President and his administration believe that genuine arms control must embrace a wide range of threats, must involve substantial reductions and real constraints, and must be effectively verifiable. A serious approach requires no less.

Compliance is critically important for real arms control. The Soviets and their allies have employed chemical weapons, in violation of existing accords, in Southeast Asia and Afghanistan; they have violated the arms-control provisions of the Helsinki Accords; and the Administration, which will be reporting to the Congress on the evidence and findings involved, also has very serious concerns about Soviet compliance with other arms-control commitments, such as the ABM and SALT treaties. [Note: The President provided reports to the Congress in January 1984 and February 1985 on the increasing pattern of Soviet non-compliance with arms-control agreements including the ABM Treaty and SALT II.] Such problems of Soviet non-compliance, like the Soviet military buildup and projection of military power throughout the globe during what was to be a period of "détente" in the 1970s, must sober us profoundly. But they must also strengthen our resolve to maintain modern and credible deterrent forces and to seek arms control that enhances rather than diminishes U.S. security and global stability.

Those who work in the present administration believe that arms control embraces many types of forces, including nuclear, conventional, and chemical. We believe in reduction to equal, far lower levels of forces, not in legitimizing buildups or current imbalances. We affirm the defensive character of our Western alliances. Our commitment to serious negotiations in support of these principles is strong and will not be shaken by temporary setbacks, including Soviet threats to walk away from negotiation tables. We insist only that negotiations produce real reductions and real constraints, that they be equitable, and that they include effective verification provisions that help insure their viability.

Above all, this administration seeks to deter nuclear war and believes that deterrence of war and strengthening of peace requires both sufficient military strength to maintain the balance and sound negotiations built on sound criteria, not on illusions about freezes or unilateral disarmament. I have personally witnessed the President in discussions wherein he recalls American experiences in the Second World War, in Anzio, Normandy, and the Pacific. He remembers the casualties we took and the terrible decisions that had to be made. When the President stated before the United Nations General Assembly that a nuclear war cannot ever be won and must never be fought, he meant what he said. He and his administration are determined to avoid the tragedy of war.

The charge that the current U.S. government is not serious about arms control and world peace is simply wrong. President Reagan has gone much further in his initiatives for genuine arms reductions than his predecessors. He has proposed a 50 per cent cut in ballistic missiles and a one-third cut in their warheads, a zero option on intermediate-range land-based missiles, a comprehensive ban on chemical weapons, tightened nuclear testing verification, conventional force reductions, and extensive confidence-building measures. These are concrete and genuine arms-control proposals, and they are accompanied by specific proposals to resolve regional conflicts and encourage progress in human rights and economic well-being. This administration would be delighted to see progress in any and all of the current negotiations, or to engage in others of serious merit.

The United States has made progress in several of the arms-control negotiations and is determined to make more. But to continue to make progress, it needs the understanding and support of its own informed citizens and of its allies, just as our Western partners need the understanding and support of their own people.

If democratic governments can have the trust of the people whose values they share and reflect and are willing to defend with real strength and persistence, then we are assured of future progress toward a more secure world on a basis that is both realistic and ethical.

POSTSCRIPT: 1985 DEVELOPMENTS

In November 1983 the Soviets walked out of the Geneva START and INF negotiations. Subsequently, the United States repeatedly sought to persuade the Soviet Union to renew the negotiations. Following President Reagan's invitation to Soviet Foreign Minister Andrei Gromyko to visit Washington in September 1984, diplomatic contacts led to the Thanksgiving Day 1984 announcement that the United States and the Soviet Union had agreed to enter into new negotiations on "the whole range of questions" concerning nuclear offensive arms and defensive and space arms, and that Secretary of State Shultz and Foreign Minister Gromyko would discuss these questions in Geneva on January 7-8, 1985.

The joint statement issued at the conclusion of the Geneva meeting on January 8, 1985, noted that new negotiations would address "a complex of questions concerning space and nuclear arms—both strategic and intermediate-range—with these questions considered and resolved in their interrelationship." In addition the two sides agreed that the "objective of the negotiations will be to work out effective agreements aimed at preventing an arms race in space and terminating it on earth, and at strengthening strategic stability." Secretary Shultz affirmed the President's hope that these negotiations will ultimately "lead to the complete elimination of nuclear arms everywhere."

The United States and the Soviet Union began the new negotiations on March 12, 1985, in Geneva. Both countries agreed that the negotiations would be conducted by a delegation from each side divided into three groups: strategic offensive nuclear arms, intermediate-range nuclear forces (INF), and defense and space arms issues.

With respect to *strategic arms*, the United States seeks radical reductions in the numbers and destructive power of strategic forces and is prepared to explore tradeoffs that would accommodate differences in the two sides' force structures. The United States also seeks the elimination of, or radical reductions in, U.S. and Soviet *intermediate-range nuclear forces* and is prepared to build upon the flexibility in its previous position (fall 1983) in pursuit of the lowest possible equal global limits.

The *defense and space* negotiations will include questions of space arms (whether based on earth or in space) and the broader question of strategic defense, including existing Soviet defenses. In the near term, the United States wishes to reverse the erosion in the stability of the strategic relationship that has resulted both from Soviet actions in violation of the spirit and letter of the Anti-Ballistic-Missile (ABM) Treaty and from the continuing growth in Soviet offensive nuclear forces. The United States intends to raise the issues of ground- and space-based systems. Looking to the longer term, the United States will discuss the possibility of moving away from a situation in which security rests on the threat of massive nuclear retaliation toward one of increased reliance on defense to strengthen deterrence. The President's Strategic Defense Initiative is designed to explore that possibility. It is a research program fully consistent with the ABM Treaty of 1972.

The three areas of negotiation are substantively interrelated. It is the U.S. view, however, that if we can reach agreement in one or two of these negotiations, we should move ahead to implement those agreements, even if differences remain in the other areas.

There will be many tough issues to try to resolve. Nevertheless, the Administration hopes that through such negotiations we can reach agreements with the Soviet Union to reduce nuclear arsenals, strengthen stability, and increase our security and that of our allies. The United States will continue to consult closely with its allies. We will continue to press for correction in areas of Soviet non-compliance. And in diplomatic contacts with the Soviet Union we will continue to press for progress in other arms-control efforts as well as in other key areas of the U.S.-Soviet relationship, including regional problems and human rights.

CHART 1 AND CHART 2   45

CHART 1

U.S. Defense and Social Spending
as Percentage of Federal Budget

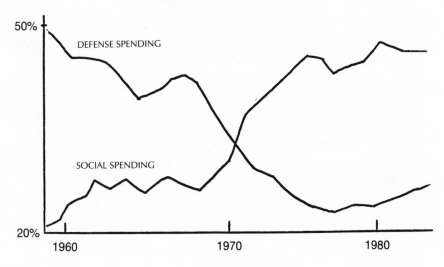

CHART 2

U.S. and Soviet Defense Spending
(Billions of Dollars*)

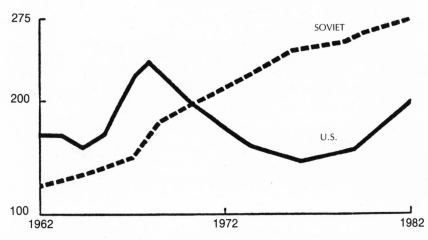

*Allowing for inflation.

CHART 3

FEDERAL BUDGET, NATIONAL DEFENSE,
AND STRATEGIC FORCES
(Billions of Constant FY 1984 Dollars)

FEDERAL BUDGET

NATIONAL DEFENSE

STRATEGIC FORCES

900 800 700 600 500 400 300 200 100 0

1950   1955   1960   1965   1970   1975   1980   1985

CHART 4   47

CHART 4

U.S. Nuclear Weapon Stockpile

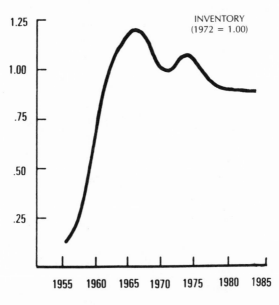

INVENTORY
(1972 = 1.00)

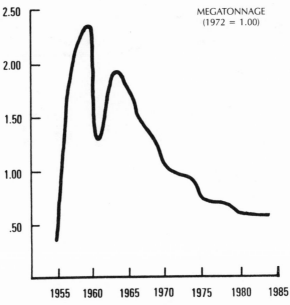

MEGATONNAGE
(1972 = 1.00)

CHART 5

U.S. and Soviet ICBM Launcher and Reentry Vehicle (RV) Deployment

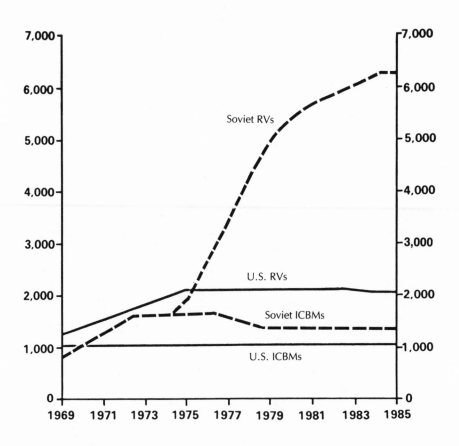

CHART 6   49

CHART 6

U.S. START PROPOSAL AND THE STRATEGIC BALANCE
Fall 1984

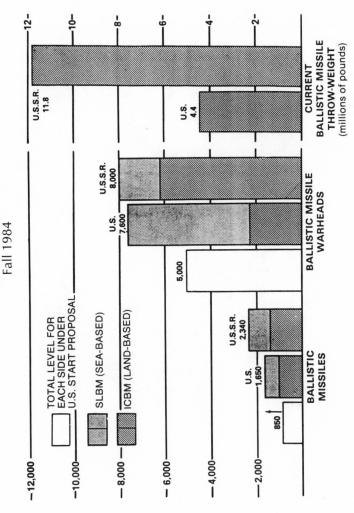

CHART 7

TARGET COVERAGE OF SOVIET SS-20
AND NATO PERSHING II AND GROUND-LAUNCHED CRUISE MISSILES

   I SS–20 location
   ▲ ICBM location

CHART 8 51

CHART 8

NATO–WARSAW PACT FORCE COMPARISON
1984

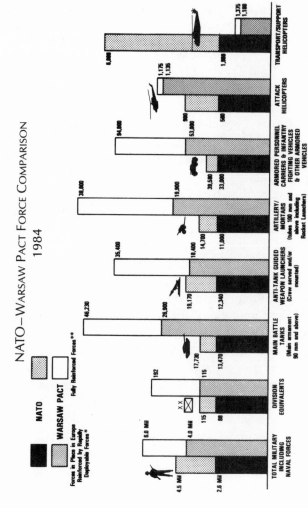

NOTE: Warsaw Pact divisions normally consist of fewer personnel than many NATO divisions but contain more tanks and artillery, thereby obtaining similar combat power.

*Rapidly deployable forces include those U.S. forces whose equipment is stored in Europe and high-readiness Soviet forces located in the Baltic, Belorussian, Carpathian, Odessa, Kiev, and North Caucasus military districts.

**Fully reinforced forces include North American reinforcements and all Warsaw Pact forces located west of the Ural Mountains.

War and Peace in the Nuclear Age

ERWIN WILKENS

WITHIN CHURCH CIRCLES TODAY there is broad agreement on certain basic questions of war and peace in the nuclear age. War can no longer be considered morally defensible as a means of policy. War waged with nuclear weapons must be repudiated because it would destroy life indiscriminately in whole regions. Universal human rights and social justice must be the foundations of a peace that cannot be established by force.

Christians can agree on these points. But we are left with the problem of how actually to secure this peace—with questions of political and military strategy, weapons technology, and military service. Opinions are divided over how far it is possible to give clear Christian opinions on these more technical matters.

In the German Evangelical Church (EKD), from which I come, a dispute over the foundations and methods of political ethics has persisted since the church's struggle with the Third Reich. Where does theology get the criteria, values, and subjects for its political ethics? How do general principles lead to particular political decisions? What importance should be given to the particular facts of a situation when applying general principles? What can be done to foster political agreement between Christians and non-Christians?

Some Christians attempt to tie political ethics as closely as possible to the faith. They search for an unequivocal Christian formula from which political programs and directions can be derived, thereby elevating these political programs to the rank of final truths and absolute certainties.

Erwin Wilkens was the theological vice president at the central office of the German Evangelical Church (EKD), a Lutheran body, and is now retired. He previously was a pastor in Hanover.

Other Christians seek to combine a biblical understanding of man and his world with rational knowledge won through experience. They believe that certainty of faith must be distinguished from certainty of action, and that the political mandate of the Christian and of the church must not be separated from an often highly complex political and ethical situation. Ethics and politics cannot claim to embody only timeless and absolute truth but, being the work of man, are attempts to put the better in place of the worse. To achieve the politically possible requires an openness to relativity.

In this dispute over the fundamentals of political ethics that has persisted since the Second World War, my church has been following the second of these conceptions. Let me formulate it again:

● Christianity cannot offer a complete theological guide to ordering the political world. Abstract ethical formulas do not provide us with specific political ends and means. Conscience must cooperate with rational consideration. Christianity must, for its political service, take into account existing political structures, instrumentalities, experiences, and modes of thought. Christian political service therefore calls for a thorough knowledge and close analysis of the world situation.

● Christianity must always have in mind, too, how it is to get its counsels heard and accepted. Since the decisions to be made are not of a kind that concerns Christians only, Christian contributions to political discourse must be convincing and even compelling to general political reason. The real strength of a Christian contribution to the course of world events lies, therefore, in the independence of judgment and in the circumspection with which aspects of a concrete case are assessed, subjected to the judgment of conscience, and factually argued.

Doctrine of the Just War

A compromise must always be sought between our obligation to peace and the right of a people to collective self-defense by force of arms. Therefore in its early days Christianity adopted the doctrine of the just war. This doctrine was based on the conviction that, in a clear case of defense, after certain restrictive criteria had been conscientiously applied, an act of war could be moral. The most important of these criteria are the principles of proportionality (the means must be proportionate to the aims) and discrimination (the use of arms must be limited to military targets). The doctrine stands or falls by the possibility of controlling warfare, making its effects calculable, and, in case of moral violations, limiting and ending it.

The doctrine of the just war is based on a model of natural law whose closed order of values covers all possible moral decisions and determines in advance, whatever the circumstances, whether something is good or evil, sinful or not sinful. But in extreme situations, decisions on war touch a perilous moral borderline. Such borderline situations cannot be wholly taken into account by a rigid, timeless doctrinal system. The moral problem of war lies in the conflict between differing and often contradictory demands on man and human society.

A rigid system is even less helpful to the Christian conscience in situations where embroilment in the guilt of the world is so evident that action is possible only under tribulation and with a belief in forgiveness. Only through faith in Christ and the obligation to love, not through adherence to the objective rules of a value system, can Christian action find its freedom and limitations.

Nonetheless, the doctrine of the just war contains indispensable moral, legal, and humanitarian elements. Yet long before the nuclear era a process of erosion had begun through which the doctrine lost its original force. In the First World War the tendency of war to become total became overwhelmingly evident. The Second World War then delivered a death-blow to the doctrine of the just war.

The shock of the use of atomic weapons on Hiroshima and Nagasaki in 1945 at first raised hopes that humanity would now make every effort to reject war as a means of solving conflicts. Disgust with violence was supplemented by the realization that this new means of mass destruction had led war to the point of absurdity.

Several attempts have been made to outlaw war as a means of policy. The charter of the League of Nations included a limited ban on war, and the Kellogg-Briand Pact of 1928 banned war altogether. In its article 1, the charter of the United Nations sets forth the preservation of world peace and security as one of its main aims. The charter obligates U.N. members to renounce any use or threat of force in international relations. It admits the right to self-defense, but only until intervention by the Security Council. In fact, however, the proscription of war as a means of policy has not yet taken root in the thinking of peoples and their governments.

In 1948 the World Council of Churches, meeting at Amsterdam, coined the lapidary phrase, "According to God's will, war shall not be." With regard to the doctrine of the just war, it added: "The traditional view that for a just cause a just war can be waged with just weapons, can under such circumstance [i.e., in view of the possibility of a total war with nuclear arms] no longer be sustained."

Ethical Dilemmas in World Politics

Quite obviously, the proscription of war as a political tactic and the abandonment of the just war doctrine did not solve the political and ethical dilemmas posed by the world situation.

Fear of a world-wide catastrophe is not irrational; no one can doubt that an unrestricted nuclear war might mean the self-destruction of mankind. The strategic concepts of flexible response, limited war, and a selective use of nuclear weapons preserve the credibility of deterrence. Together with arms-control efforts, these strategies are intended to prevent, by political means, a catastrophe that has become militarily feasible.

Peace is order of the highest positive quality, and freedom and justice are indispensable characteristics of this order. The preservation of these and other values has hitherto depended on a readiness to defend or restore them by force if need be. Most political thinking holds as fast as ever to this concept; the necessary sea-change has not yet occurred. The present dilemma is that total war makes defense impossible while the total state has destroyed pacifist ideals. The task is to steer a course between the risk of nuclear war and the renunciation of political freedom.

Christian ethics might have solved its task if an unequivocal rejection of war resulted in equally unequivocal positive conclusions. But even the World Council of Churches' Amsterdam statement of 1948 avoided such assertions. Evidently, the authors of that statement did not think that a ban on war for religious-ethical reasons and a rejection of the doctrine of the just war would result automatically in pacifism. Instead, they stressed divergences of opinion on practical issues and warned that Christians could not cease to consider "as their brethren and sisters" those who held different views.

The Amsterdam statement left a great number of questions unanswered, and we have been trying to deal with them ever since. Does rejection of war necessarily lead to rejection of all means of war and of all readiness ever to go to war? Is there an ethical difference between the threat of the use of force and the actual use of force? Should we accept the existence of armed forces as a political means of securing peace?

The discussion that has persisted in church circles since the 1950s has shown that these questions cannot be answered with abstract logic. If force may not be used to deter force under any circumstances, force may more than ever rear its head as a guiding principle. To forbid Christians to take any part in armament and deterrence would practically mean the elimination of all ethical demands on the conduct of international relations between nations. Furthermore, it is not for Christianity to impute unethical motives to a country that resists being violated by a dictatorial regime, or to disparage its will to defend itself.

Heidelberg Theses on War and Peace

Many Christians insist that it is necessary to bear witness to the faith free of all considerations about the workings of this world. But other maintain that political circumspection and regard for the laws of this world are also ethically justified. Thereby, the latter feel, the Church also safeguards its right to have a say in the political discussion.

One of the most important documents of recent decades was the 1959 Heidelberg Theses on war and peace in the nuclear age.The Heidelberg Theses leave aside the dispute between theological schools over the grounds of political ethics, preferring to proceed more empirically. They declare that peace must be maintained in the scientific-technological era, and they demand that a continuing effort be made to abolish war as a political instrument. This demand, at first sight, has a practical rather than an ethical justification. In a world increasingly interdependent, economically and otherwise, survival depends on peace, which must be safeguarded by whatever means required. This task is all embracing; simple rules that enjoin or prohibit certain actions do not suffice. Moreover, we cannot exclude the possibility that peace can be achieved only at the price of our civic liberties or through a third world war. After all, it is easier to ensure peace in an enslaved world than in a world with competing systems of government.

From an analysis of the world situation the theses draw the conclusion that mankind is tempted either to submit to slavery for fear of war or to allow war to break out for fear of slavery. They add, however, that mankind is not ready to capitulate to a dictatorial world power, all the less so because lasting peace cannot be secured in that manner anyway: the victorious power will come into conflict with itself or with the suppressed.

According to the Heidelberg Theses, two totally different conclusions may be drawn from this world situation. One party concludes that to secure peace it should renounce all weapons, while the other intends to achieve peace with liberty by possessing nuclear arms. The Heidelberg Theses say that the Church must recognize both decisions—to renounce all arms, to keep arms ready for deterrence—as valid for Christians. Approval of the possession of nuclear arms, however, is formulated restrictively: "The Church must recognize participation in the attempt to secure peace and liberty through the presence of nuclear arms as today still a possible Christian way of acting."

This thesis (the eighth of the Heidelberg Theses) has been subjected to harsh criticism, perhaps all the more so because it was incorporated into the 1981 Peace Memorandum of the German Evangelical Church. Most of the criticism disregards the fact that this eighth thesis is not an abstract construction but the result of an assessment of contradictory ethico-political and strategic demands. The phrase "today still" is not to be understood as unconditional or as an "aim in itself," as Pope John Paul II said in a comparable context. Rather, it expresses the realization that peace and freedom are guaranteed neither by the possession nor by the renunciation of nuclear armaments. Each of these positions is an attempt to avoid the risks of the other, but neither side can deny the risk implied in its own position. This thesis implies, however, that the statesmen of the governments involved will continue to work constructively at easing the armament situation.

He who rejects this thesis must work out a better overall concept and make plausible its ability to perform the present world political task better and with less danger. That task is to secure peace for all the nations of the world and, at the same time, to enable man to live in freedom, justice, and human dignity. Mere abstract postulates without regard to political reality, practical utility, and possible consequences are not what people need from the Church.

The Strategy of Deterrence

In the absence of an effective system of world peace, the tensions between the world powers will take the form of a mutual military buildup. Yet nuclear destruction of both the adversary and one's own people cannot be anybody's aim. For each side, the purpose of this arms buildup can only be to prevent the use of arms by the other side. The success of the current system of deterrence depends on reciprocity: one side's security is based on the security of the other. This fundamental understanding must not be jeopardized. Today's weapons have been reduced to deterrents—that is, they have become political weapons.

Taken by itself, the whole structure of deterrence, based on the balance of the two sides' strategic armaments, is highly complex and unstable. Armed forces are credible as a deterrent only if they create significant risks for the aggressor. Each side's credibility is based on its resolve to use its defensive potential.

More pointedly, the defending side must be resolved to do what it may not do morally, in the conviction that it then will not have to do it. This paradox reflects the political disgrace of the world powers, which have so far refused to cooperate responsibly in solving mankind's urgent problems. Until they do so, there is no chance of arriving at an unambiguous ethical thesis or solving the dilemma solely on the basis of armaments. It should also be said that there is no real difference between conventional weapons and nuclear weapons; anyone who declares nuclear arms to be a crime against mankind must include all other weaponry in this statement.

We live in a transitory situation of crisis management, and our ethical evaluation is likewise transitory. This situation is bearable only if the aim is an effective peace order. Christianity must make clear the fact that it does not accept the present state of affairs as permanent. As Pope John Paul II told the United Nations in 1982:

> Under current conditions, deterrence based on balance—certainly not as an end in itself, but as a step on the way toward a progressive disarmament—may still be judged morally acceptable. Nonetheless, in order to ensure the peace, it is indispensable not to be satisfied with this minimum which is always susceptible to the real danger of explosion.

Exactly the same thought is expressed in the EKD's 1981 Peace Memorandum:

> If the reprieve still given for securing peace politically is not used to disrupt the sequence of rearmament measures, there will come a time when the scandal and the risk of the armament spiral will weigh heavier than the benefit of the system of deterrence.

The Priority of Politics

The relation between politics and military armaments must be adjusted to give priority to the political dimension. Armaments are a symptom rather than a cause of the threat to world peace. An effective peace movement will therefore have to broaden the discussion beyond the issues of armaments to the whole area of politics.

War is not an inferior form of politics but rather a failure of politics. Wrong policies, not arms, are what lead to war. To want to secure peace through arms reductions is therefore not enough. Arms buildups, of course, are even less likely to secure peace.

Whether we strive for the renunciation of arms or for improvements in deterrence, we must have a clear conception of what the political future is to look like. Current discussions of peace typically lack a careful assessment of the complex world situation, which is largely determined by the two superpowers. Rivalry between the Soviet Union and the United States overlies the tensions at other focal points of world politics. The ideological principles and political behavior of the USSR are irritating, often ambiguous, and contradictory. They spring from the mixture of inferiority sentiments and the need to feel superior that pervades the whole Soviet system. It is, as everybody knows, a very dangerous mixture. On the other hand, the USSR clearly has the ability to assess its own domestic and foreign policy risks. Its policy of expansion should be answered by the West with quiet determination. On this point, some critical questions could be addressed to the policy of the United States.

In attempting to broaden the discussion of peace beyond the narrow fixation on the armament question, we should seek closer cooperation between the Protestant and Catholic churches. Papal statements like the following offer a suitable basis for such cooperation:

> I am indeed deeply convinced that, in view of the scientifically predicted consequences of an atomic war, there is only one morally and humanely acceptable decision: to reduce the atomic weapons, in the expectation of their future complete abolishment, by way of explicit agreements and the obligation for effective mutual control by both sides [speech in Rome, December 13, 1981].

As far as possible the churches should avoid getting involved in detailed questions of strategy and weapons, but they must be allowed to speak up as critical observers, sometimes warning, sometimes encouraging.

To reduce armaments and secure peace requires cooperation among the nations. Neither a balance of arms, nor mutual deterrence, nor moral appeals, nor unilateral renunciation can succeed in keeping the peace, if we do not all work together in the belief that nuclear war must never happen.

A Crisis of Faith

RICHARD JOHN NEUHAUS

THE CURRENT DEBATE over nuclear weaponry is skewed by its conception of peace as solely the avoidance of war. That definition of peace gives no place to what the American bishops' Pastoral Letter on War and Peace called "the good and the true and the honorable," those values by which we live. The question is not simply "how do we prevent war?," even nuclear war, as urgent as that question is. It is, rather, how do we live in fidelity to those values, those good and true and honorable ways of ordering human life with justice? We have inherited these values, and we are responsible not only to preserve but also—God willing—to extend them, to give other persons in other parts of the world and in other generations an opportunity to carry on what is still the most daring and fresh and exciting experiment in the ordering of human life, the experiment of democracy.

Contrary to this, antithetical to it, is the mere concern for survival. In the sundry "peace movements," the prime dynamic is fear and the prime goal is survival.

The bible of the nuclear freeze movement in the United States is Jonathan Schell's *The Fate of the Earth*. Schell is candid in saying that the only issue is survival, not simply whether we survive as individuals but whether the human race will survive. It is assumed in the modern world, he says, that there is nothing beyond life as we know it, no larger world of which our world is a part, no transcendent meanings that can survive nuclear holocaust. The nuclear holocaust would be the end of meaning itself.

Though intellectually defensible, this position is obviously incompatible with biblical faith. For the churches, the current debate over

Richard John Neuhaus, a Lutheran pastor, is director of the Center on Religion and Society, located in New York. He is the author of nine books and many articles on theology, ethics, and social change.

nuclear war is not primarily over matters of parity and balance and sufficiency and the like. It is a crisis of faith, of whether we still believe what for 2,000 years at least the catholic tradition has declared to be the meaning of the human drama within the eternal purposes of God.

Lack of a Normative Ethic

In our public discourse it has become extremely difficult to discuss even the possibility of a normative ethic that may go beyond immediate satisfaction and the passion for survival. This was brilliantly articulated by Alasdair MacIntyre in his disturbing book *After Virtue*. MacIntyre shows, with great philosophical sophistication, that Western intellectual life has largely reached the point at which we not only cannot agree upon a normative ethic but cannot even agree on a point of reference by which we might discuss normative ethics. Moral philosophy has become simply the ethics of personal preference. "You should not do this" or "you should do that" is regularly translated as simply, "I prefer that you do not do this," or "I prefer that you do that." My preference is as valid as your preference. Therefore we do not talk about the truth, because we do not believe that anybody possesses or can possess the truth.

We have not grasped the very bad news until we understand that the churches have largely capitulated to this abandonment of ethical discourse. Far from contributing to the public debate or elevating its level, the churches have increasingly become instruments of delegitimation—to use a sociological term—of the very idea of moral discourse. No longer confident of the ethics they once proclaimed, derived from the faith they once held, the Christian communities have sought legitimation and significance by becoming actors within the chief idolatry of our time: politics—that is, politics under the umbrella and control of the modern state.

This is the crisis of faith.

Can those values that we associate with the democratic experiment be not only sustained but revitalized? Not without a theological and a moral reconstruction that will for the first time ground the democratic experiment in biblical faith.

The sources of the democratic experiment were marginal to or even hostile to Christian faith. The four primary sources of democratic theory are the classical Greek tradition, the Cromwellian English tradition, the French revolutionary tradition, and the American tradition. In the Cromwellian and the American traditions, democratic theory was derived from a somewhat marginal theological tradition within the Christian community: in the American case, deistic (but a deistic tradition vaguely comfortable with popular democratic public affirmation and belief), and in the Cromwellian, from what we Lutherans call the left wing of the Reformation.

Never in the last 200 years has it been articulated persuasively within the Christian community that the fundamental notions of democracy—of the dignity of the human person, therefore of the necessary limits of the state, of the discrete spheres of influence of economic, political, and cultural life—are rooted in Christianity. These foundational notions of democracy have not been theologized persuasively and have not entered into the belief-system of the faithful.

This I take to be the great intellectual, theological, and ethical task of the next several decades. Upon this task depend all the issues that engage us in the nuclear debate. Upon it depends the possibility of believably saying to another generation, or even to this generation, that here are values that are not simply *our* preferences, as opposed to the preferences of others, nor simply the habits of life that we consider more orderly or more efficient or in some other way superior. Subjective arguments for defending democracy are not sufficient when people are asked to be willing to surrender their own lives or to take the lives of others in the defense of democratic values.

Views of America's Role

There is today a pervasive disillusionment with the idea that America in any way represents a hope or a promise with which we must keep faith. Abraham Lincoln's phrase about America as the last, best hope of earth seems hubristic and arrogant to a lot of people. Far from being possessed of a notion of "manifest destiny," many Americans, especially among that elite called the "new class," are thoroughly demoralized to the point of holding an opposite view of America's role.

In 1982 the Roper public-opinion organization surveyed teachers of ethics, theology, and religious studies in our seminaries and divinity schools. Among the assertions tested was this:"On balance and considering the alternatives, American democracy is a force for good in the world." Barely half of those who are preparing students for professional ministries in American religion believe that assertion is true. A fourth think it is false, and the others are unsure.

There have also been informal surveys among the bureaucrats within the "church and society" departments at mainline Protestant churches. At 475 Riverside Drive in New York (the headquarters of the National Council of Churches and several of its member denominations), it is estimated that less than 15 per cent of the leadership of the churches' public witness in the liberal-ecumenical Protestant denominations would argue that on balance and considering the alternatives, American democracy is a force for good in the world. As many as 50 to 60 per cent would endorse the opposite position—that American democracy is a force for evil in the world, a prime cause of injustice. And at the heart of the American democratic experiment, they will quickly add, is of course the corruption of capitalism, the beast eating away at the very entrails of any hope for a more promising human future.

These views do not represent American popular opinion or the convictions of the great majority of church people in America. Such views do, however, have an inordinate influence in shaping the public witness and political engagement of the mainline churches.

Attempts at an American Public Philosophy

The historic American belief in some kind of mission, some special obligation to humankind, in being the "city on the hill," has long been discredited in fashionable academic and intellectual circles. For many younger people, Vietnam swept that notion away.

Today one of the few theologians who are attempting to defend that idea of mission is Wolfhart Pannenberg of the University of Munich. In a little book called *Human Nature, Election, and History* he dares to suggest that the idea of historical election might still be valid for trying to understand the responsibility of nations, and specifically of the United States, in the world today. Regrettably, Pannenberg is a voice crying in the wilderness on this point. Unless the American sense of identity and purpose can be grounded theologically and religiously, it will lack moral credibility with the American people.

Attempts within this century to construct a public philosophy for the American experiment have been numerous and in some cases distinguished. Walter Lippmann is perhaps the person most commonly associated with the notion of a public philosophy during the first half of this century. After the Second World War, Arthur M. Schlesinger, Jr., solidly centered in the liberal community, tried to develop an idea of "the vital center," again an attempt at an American public philosophy, particularly over against the lures of Marxist-Leninist totalitarianism. The difficulty with these efforts is that they did not ground their arguments in—or even allude to—the actual belief-system of the American people, which is overwhelmingly and explicitly Judeo-Christian.

The Jesuit John Courtney Murray, in a magisterial way that I still find persuasive (indeed awesome and monumental in its implications), tried to develop a theological grounding for what he called the American proposition. On the Protestant side, the Niebuhr brothers, H. Richard and the better known Reinhold, aimed at a similar goal. Today, our crisis is such that in theological and social-ethical circles it is considered dangerously cold-war-like, if not reactionary, to refer to Murray and Niebuhr. Yet unless that enterprise in which these thinkers were engaged is revived for our time, I place very little confidence in the popular willingness to defend democratic values and to keep faith with our heritage, and therefore extremely little confidence in any military measures aimed at compensating for that moral default.

I am not suggesting that it is the primary mission of the Church to firm up or to legitimate democratic governments. The Christian Church has existed under many different forms of government. And yet I believe that at this moment in history there is a theologically and biblically grounded imperative to recognize the stake that the Church has in democracy.

Consider two simple linkages. I think that the ministry of John Paul II is of critical importance in the first linkage—that between the notion of the person and the idea of freedom. This is a theological and an ethical linkage. It is normative. The second linkage is more descriptive: In our world, recognition of the human person and of the exercise of the person's responsible freedom in community is respected only by those regimes that claim to be or aspire to be democratic. That, it seems to me, is simply a matter of fact—undeniable.

The conclusion to draw from this observed fact is a prudential one: It is not only in the interest of the Church but *obligatory* for the Church to do all it can to advance the prospects of that kind of government which respects our Christ-based understanding of the human person and the exercise of responsible freedom, individually and communally.

The Churches' Role in the Political Process

The churches in America that are trying to address the underlying questions in the nuclear debate are badly divided. There is a common understanding that in a democracy the Church as an institution and individual members of the Church are political actors. But there are profound disagreements as to how the Church should act collectively.

In the past, the mainstream liberal, ecumenical Protestant denominations have been the primary spokesmen for Christian perspectives on the moral consequences of public policy. Today, however, the Roman Catholic Church, the large community of evangelicals, the 20 million or so who claim to be Lutherans, and the very substantial and militant group of fundamentalists known as the religious right are all engaged more or less directly in trying to influence public discourse and public policy.

One interpretation of the significance of the U.S. Catholic bishops' pastoral letter on nuclear arms suggests that the bishops intended to present an ultimatum to the American government: If you do not change your policy radically, then we will directly intervene in the political process in order to exercise political power, and radically undo your political decisions. That interpretation is wrong. Such an ultimatum would signify exactly the triumphalism that since Vatican II, Roman Catholicism has rightly abjured as one of the past sins of the church. When John Paul I became pope for those tragically few days, he broke with precedent by setting aside the tiara, which was the last vestige of the Catholic Church's triumphalistic symbolism about direct political rule. John Paul II followed that good precedent.

I believe that the setting aside of the tiara, not only by Roman Catholics but by everybody else—the National Council of Churches, the Moral Majority, the Christian Action Council—is one of the most hopeful signs for the Church. As long as we are wearing or attempting to wear some kind of tiara, trying to find our influence and our meaning, our significance, by being institutional actors in the games of Caesar played by the rules of Caesar, we will bring the Church into discredit. And we will, ironically, destroy the positive influence we can have as Christians, individually and corporately, in bringing the mandates of the Gospel and the wisdom of our Western tradition to bear upon momentous public issues of our time.

We have to dare to say no to the imperiousness of politics and the modern state. We have to have the nerve to appear irrelevant in talking about the spiritual kingdom, in believing that prayer is finally of greater consequence than whatever games we might play, no matter how effectively, within the arena of Caesar. We need a more radical movement. To be a Christian is to be engaged in the adventure of seeking to live by courage, truth, honor, and a profound sense of the dignity of the human person that is God's own gift. It is to be joyously, and sometimes painfully, out of step with all other ways of understanding peace. As the Apostle Paul says, the peace of Christ surpasses our understanding.

The German Churches Speak Out

WOLFHART PANNENBERG

THE POPULAR MOVEMENT against the deployment of additional
missiles in Western European countries is closely connected
with a deep and widespread disappointment over the collapse of
détente. Europeans had experienced the easing of tensions during
the seventies with particular relief, since it was they who had
suffered most from the confrontation of the two world powers on
their continent—and in the case of Germany, in their own country.
They are therefore extremely reluctant to give up all hope for
détente. This mentality leads many to play down the importance of
increased Soviet armament while at the same time objecting to any
development on the Western side that could aggravate political
tensions.

Opposition to nuclear armament has been around since the late
forties, when the Göttingen physicists urged their fellow physicists
not to take part in the further development of nuclear weapons.
During the fifties, Easter marches were held in many European
cities to protest nuclear armament. Those marches drew only a
very slight minority of the population and did not have much impact
on the general public. During the sixties this opposition became
even more marginal, overshadowed by the Vietnam controversy
and, later, by the prospect of détente between the superpowers.

In recent years the opposition to nuclear armament has gained
not only new vigor but also a new character. On the surface, there
is disbelief that détente came to an end because of the Soviet military
buildup and Soviet political gains in Asia and Africa. People are
unwilling to believe that the promise of a continuing easing of
tensions was deceptive. What has therefore developed is a dispo-

Wolfhart Pannenberg is a noted Protestant theologian who teaches systematic
theology at the University of Munich, where he is also head of the Ecumenical
Institute.

sition to criticize American activities, and especially the policies of the Reagan administration, wherever these seem to go against the grain of détente. A widespread distrust of American policies has emerged, which is a new element in a relationship hitherto marked by a high degree of confidence. There is a feeling that Western Europe is threatened not only by a potential adversary but also, if unintentionally, by a powerful ally. European confidence in the competence and rationality of American leadership of the Western alliance has eroded.

A PERCEPTION OF WESTERN WEAKNESS

Behind this change in popular opinion in some European countries, especially West Germany, there seems to be a perception of Western weakness, a feeling that the balance of power has slowly but steadily shifted to the disadvantage of the West. Martin Kriele, a professor of constitutional law at the University of Cologne, has identified a subconscious perception of this shift as the underlying basis of the new attitude, though it rarely enters the argument explicitly.

Kriele dates the European perception of a shift in the balance of power from the Vietnam war, and certainly that war—or, more precisely, the loss of Vietnam by the United States despite extensive efforts to save it—was a watershed in the awareness of many Europeans. For me, however, a sense of erosion in the American position had begun much earlier. During the Soviet coup in Czecho- slovakia in 1948, the United States either was not able or did not see fit to respond in such a way as to protect its own interests or the political freedom of the Czech people. Europeans experienced a similar sense of American inactivity during the events in East Germany in 1953 and in Hungary in 1956, which were followed by a long series of similar setbacks all the way to the Afghanistan crisis of 1981. The loss of Vietnam was not therefore an isolated event. It changed the perception of the balance of power more than the others, however, because in this case the United States had com- mitted itself to halting Communist expansion and failed to do so.

I agree with Kriele that (1) the new fear of war arises not so much from the actual existence of nuclear weapons as from a perceived erosion of Western political power that renders the deterrence policies of the past less effective, and that (2) there is a tendency to condone the atrocities of the ascendant power while focusing moral judgment on what appears to be the losing side. This may not be very fair, but I suspect it is a way of excusing oneself for seeking some form of settlement with the ascendant power. The now fashionable term for this is "security partnership." While security partnerships were developed among the Western nations in the past in order to discourage potential adversaries, the term now refers to a settlement with a potential adversary so as to reduce the risk of a confrontation.

In a situation of perceived instability, a serious effort by the inferior power to redress the balance of power inevitably creates an increased sense of insecurity, since the reaction of the other side is incalculable. I think this feeling is very widespread in Germany and in some other European countries because of the deployment of additional nuclear missiles. The concern is not so much that the new missiles on the Western side are a threat in themselves, though some certainly see them that way, but that the reaction of the other side is incalculable.

Comments by some members of the current U.S. administration about "limited nuclear war" gave further cause for concern. Until then, people had assumed that nuclear deterrence would operate to avoid *any* kind of war. Central Europe would be the likely place for a "limited nuclear war," and whether it could be contained to that region or not would not make much difference to the German people. These comments have presumably served to increase public support for the so-called peace movement against the deployment of additional American missiles.

The new awareness that deterrence could fail and that nuclear war could become a real possibility was intensified by the deployment of Pershing II missiles in West Germany, not only because those missiles would become the primary targets of Soviet strikes, but also because of the extremely short time they allow for warning, consultation, and decision in a military confrontation. It is true that this problem of short reaction time arose first with Soviet deployment of the SS-20. But the argument against deploying Pershing IIs on the Western side in response is, as Oscar Lafontaine presented it in *Der Spiegel*, that so far there has been no inducement on the Russian side to *use* those weapons in the event of conflict. The situation will change with the deployment of similar weapons on the Western side. Lafontaine, a leading spokesman for the left-wing Social Democrats in Western Germany, is concerned that in such a situation either side could make an irrevocable decision to retaliate on the basis of mistaken information. In short, a mistake could lead to disastrous effects that neither side desired.

As a consequence of his analysis, Lafontaine demands the withdrawal of West Germany from the NATO alliance in order to restore national sovereignty on questions involving the survival of the whole nation. This sovereignty has been lost because nuclear arms can now be delivered to their targets so quickly that there might not be time for consultations between national governments, as required by the Atlantic Treaty, before a decision to retaliate is made. In calling for the restoration of national sovereignty, Lafontaine and his allies look upon the France of De Gaulle as a model. His argument, however, has met with considerable resistance not only from the Liberals (Free Democrats) and Christian Democrats but also from leading members of his own party. Hans Apel, a former minister of defense in Helmut Schmidt's government, has argued that a decision to leave NATO would hardly do away with nuclear weapons, and that the chief effect of such a decision would be to deprive West Germany of any influence on the decisions of its allies. In addition, Germany would lose any claim to protection by the Western powers.

THE CHURCHES AND NUCLEAR ARMS

The political discussion described here forms the context for the nuclear arms discussions that are taking place in West German churches. Erhard Eppler, a leading figure in the German "peace movement," was asked whether the movement would falter after the new nuclear missiles had been deployed in West Germany. He answered that he did not think so, because the movement is now deeply rooted in the country's Protestant churches.

The Catholic bishops in Germany by and large agree with the American bishops in their evaluation and criticism of the deployment of new nuclear weapons. While the production and deployment of nuclear weapons for purposes of deterrence is seen to be "still" acceptable, their actual use in combat is considered morally wrong. The difficulty with this distinction seems to be that deterrence can no longer be effective if use of the weapons is excluded a priori. Nor would military training with such weapons make any sense.

Nevertheless, a similar viewpoint has begun to prevail in the Protestant churches. Some of them even reject the political use of nuclear weapons for deterrence. In 1962 the German Reformed Church declared resistance to nuclear armaments a matter of *status confessionis*, that is, a binding religious obligation. This declaration seemed to imply a call for unilateral nuclear disarmament and aroused considerable discussion. The Evangelical Church in Germany (EKD) did not accept the Reformed suggestion that participation in nuclear defense would be contrary to the confession of the Christian Church. In a 1981 memorandum on peace, the EKD reiterated the position it had reached in the fifties and contended that nuclear deterrence is "still an acceptable strategy." Following the 1983 Vancouver Assembly of the World Council of Churches, however, the EKD declared that deterrence cannot be "forever" an acceptable means for securing peace.

The EKD has not yet called for unilateral nuclear disarmament but recommends a negotiated reduction in nuclear arms and a shifting of the focus of defense policies to conventional weapons. In view of the West's present inferiority in conventional armaments, however, such a shift would entail an enormous increase in military spending and could not help affecting the character of public life. These consequences, certainly unwanted, have not been adequately considered by most of those who favor a balance in conventional armaments instead of nuclear deterrence.

In its Vancouver statement, the World Council of Churches went much further than the German churches by declaring "production and deployment" of nuclear arms to be a "crime against humanity" and by rejecting the very idea of nuclear deterrence, which it called "immoral."

ISSUES RAISED BY CHURCH STATEMENTS

Although the theory of just war has a long standing in the Christian tradition, there is, in my opinion, no such thing as a just war. The traditional theory does not sufficiently recognize the gap between the good reasons one may have for waging war and the intrinsic dynamics of war itself. One may have just and legitimate reasons for recourse to weapons, but because of the built-in tendency toward total destruction and elimination of the enemy, no war has ever been just. The longer a war continues, the more the annihilation of the enemy becomes the dominant concern of both sides.

Therefore I strongly recommend a revision of the traditional theory of just war. The churches should never have provided a good conscience to any political party or nation that is in a state of war. Although there may be—and there certainly have been in the past—legitimate reasons for taking up arms, the consequences of such a decision get more and more out of control of the parties. The kinds of atrocities that can hardly be avoided once war is begun should never be justified.

This demand for revising the traditional theory of just war refers not only to Roman Catholic doctrine but also to the Protestant conception of a just war as a somewhat extended police action. The basic distinction between a war and a police action is that a police action is, or at least should be, a controlled action, while war has a tendency to get out of control. Because of this inherent tendency, all the good reasons for taking up arms cannot justify the war itself.

The World Council's Vancouver Statement

Given this position I have no problem with the statement of the World Council of Churches at Vancouver that no nuclear war can be a just war. Nevertheless, whether it is legitimate to use nuclear weapons in certain situations is quite a different question. Nobody can overlook the enormous difference between the destructive potential of nuclear weapons and that of conventional weapons. But the difference is one of extent of destruction, not of kind. For a human being to be wounded, to feel pain, to die, because of the use of weapons, is essentially the same whether the weapon is nuclear or non-nuclear. I cannot see a difference in principle on this point. Therefore, I cannot agree with the World Council of Churches that the production and deployment of nuclear weapons and their political use as a deterrent is morally wrong and a crime against humanity under all circumstances. I think a more carefully worked out approach is necessary. Nuclear weapons may be considered morally wrong in themselves, but so is any other weapon designed for war. In a world of highly armed and threatening powers, however, it is not immoral to resist the temptation of unilateral disarmament in favor of a negotiated settlement that would create an incomparably more secure situation than unilateral disarmament could achieve.

It is true that Jesus said, "Do not resist the evil one" (Matt. 5:39). The wisdom of these words is that resistance often results in more violence and, especially, that retaliation is likely to perpetuate violence. But this counsel refers primarily to private behavior rather than political action. I do not argue that one can completely separate private behavior from political action, but still there is a difference to be considered, since political officers act in the service of God when they "execute his wrath on the wrongdoer" (Rom. 13:4) in order to protect the life of the citizens. Another teaching of Jesus, also from the Sermon on the Mount, lends itself more easily to political action as well as individual life: "Come to terms with your opponent while you are still on the way with him" (Matt. 5:25). With these words Jesus recommends a strategy of negotiation for the settlement of disputes, rather than the use of force.

The Call for Negotiation

This prudent advice leads me to the next point. Since there is an intrinsic inhumanity in *any* use of destructive weapons, the Evangelical Church in Germany and other churches, including the Roman Catholic Church, are right in urging negotiated disarmament and an end to the arms race.

I realize, of course, that this is no new strategy, and I hope my fellow theologians are also aware that to recommend a negotiated settlement sounds somewhat glib or trite. It is a strategy that the whole world would like to see succeed, the only question being the terms of the settlement. Nevertheless, the call for negotiation is sound, and it is necessary to voice this call in order to encourage the patience required for the process of negotiation, to help keep the parties from wearying of their endeavors before they reach agreement. The urgent need of obtaining an agreement should also be addressed to all the parties concerned, lest it be understood as pressure on only one side to compromise at the conference table.

With respect to the content of an acceptable agreement on disarmament, the declaration of the Evangelical Church in Germany in support of a nuclear freeze seems unsatisfactory because it is not sufficiently qualified.The declaration explicitly states that such a freeze should apply to "all powers equally," but it does not adequately deal with the problem that a freeze would serve to legitimate and therefore to perpetuate the current imbalance of power. The document says that a freeze should become the turning point toward nuclear disarmament rather than preserving the present imbalance. But I do not see how the freeze recommended by the document could avoid bringing about precisely that unwanted result.

The EKD declaration also seems objectionable in quoting without critical qualification the WCC Vancouver statement to the effect that the churches should intensify their efforts to induce their national governments not only to proceed on the road toward a negotiated settlement but also "to turn away from projects of deploying in Europe additional or new nuclear weapons." In view of the Soviet buildup that has been going on for a number of years while the Western powers did not modernize or expand their nuclear arsenals, this statement is onesidedly directed to the West.

True Peace: Based on Justice

The Vancouver declaration begins by asserting that peace is more than simply the absence of war. According to the prophet Isaiah (2:3-4), true peace is peace based on justice. This is a point of fundamental importance in dealing with the issues raised by the so-called peace movement. (I say "so-called" because peace is by no means exclusively the concern of those committed to that particular movement.)

The prophet did not think that nations could attain peace simply by laying down their weapons. He therefore addressed himself to the reasons for armament and implied that conflicting interpretations of justice, conflicting claims to justice among the nations, lead to war. He then argued that conflict and war among nations would come to an end only when they agreed on one another's legal claims. That would require a common standard of justice. Therefore the prophet foresaw a future when disputes over conflicting legal claims would be resolved on the basis of the law of the God of Israel. Acceptance of that law, according to Isaiah, is the necessary precondition for the achievement of lasting peace.

If people agree on a common basis of legal norms in order to resolve their conflicting claims, peace will be the natural consequence; and because there will no longer be a reason for war, there will be no further use for weapons. That is the point of the well-known verse quoted again and again by followers of the "peace movement," about turning swords into plowshares and spears into pruning hooks.

The situation envisioned by the prophet, however, is utterly different from that of our present world. The powers of this world are far from accepting the law of the God of Israel as the basis for settling disputes. Therefore, the conflicting claims of politics lead again and again to the brink of war, if not to war itself. What can be done in such a situation? Is the eschatological vision of the prophet applicable, or is it simply too far removed from the political structure of the present world?

Perhaps some approximation to his vision is possible if we follow the advice of Jesus already quoted: "Come to terms with your opponent while you are still on the way with him." A negotiated settlement will usually represent a compromise rather than the ultimate justice of the law of God. Such compromises are rarely, if ever, completely satisfactory to all parties, and they often contain the roots of later conflicts. But still, a compromise that is acceptable to both parties because one party's sacrifices match those of the other party achieves some degree of mutuality and therefore some legal status. It is a precarious form of justice, to be sure, and therefore it is but a precarious form of peace. But compared to the peace of domination and oppression, it is the most desirable form of peace to be obtained in this world.

The U.S. Catholic Bishops
and Nuclear Arms

J. BRYAN HEHIR

EARLY IN *The Challenge of Peace*, the pastoral letter focusing on nuclear arms, the U.S. Catholic bishops talk about a "new moment" in the nuclear age.[1] They are not referring to the appearance of new weapons technology or new political tension between East and West. What they mean, rather, is the increased public awareness about questions of nuclear strategy and the fragility of international relations in the nuclear age, and the intensified public demand that something be done about it.

There are two levels of public debate about war and peace, and at each level there is something new. One level is broad-based, nontechnical in its approach, but very visibly a part of the argument. This level of debate is typified today by the freeze movement. The idea of a freeze, whether right or wrong as a policy prescription, engages people in the discussion of nuclear policy at the grass-roots level. A major strength of the freeze movement is that it started in town meetings in Vermont and New Hampshire and in city council meetings in California, and stimulated discussion at the local rather than national level.

This popular level of the public debate can be called new in the sense that it democratizes the nuclear issue, engaging the attention of people who have never thought or talked about it before in a sustained way.

The second level of debate is the policy level. The policy debate has gone on systematically for forty years, and its literature is voluminous. But I think it is possible to talk about a new moment

J. Bryan Hehir is secretary of the Department of Social Development and World Peace at the U.S. Catholic Conference, Washington, D.C. He was the chief advisor to the bishops' drafting committee for the 1983 pastoral letter on nuclear arms. He is the author of many works on theology and defense policy.

at this level of the debate also. One of its characteristics over four decades has been a strongly consensual character. Changing from a Democratic to a Republican and back to a Democratic administration caused only marginal changes in American nuclear policy. Certain premises were accepted as, in a sense, unarguable in the strategic debate.

Pressure on the Policy Consensus

Today the consensus is under pressure, even from some of the people who helped shape it. I will cite three among numerous examples. The first is the "no first use" article by Bundy, McNamara, Kennan, and Smith.[2] Here are four people of considerable stature and experience in the policy debate saying that NATO ought to change its fundamental premise. It's a little as if the Pope had announced that we ought to rethink the Nicene Creed—it tends to shake the system a bit!

The second example: In an article in the *Washington Post* on March 6, 1983, Maxwell Taylor, former chairman of the Joint Chiefs of Staff, argued that the way to solve the "window of vulnerability" problem was *not* to build the MX but to take out all the land-based missiles in the United States, no matter what the Soviets did.

Now, the land-sea-air triad has been one of those "untouchable" premises in American strategic doctrine. For the former chairman of the Joint Chiefs of Staff to argue that we ought to move away from it, no matter what the Soviets do, because it simply is no longer functional—this is certainly another sign of pressure on the consensus.

The third example is the Scowcroft report, whose leading conclusion is that we ought to deploy a certain number of MX missiles.[3] Hidden away—well, not really hidden away—is the secondary conclusion that what has been the major trend in American land-based missiles over the last ten years ought not to be continued—that we ought to move back from land-based MIRVs to single-warhead missiles.[4] Essentially, the Scowcroft report says—gently, no doubt—that the major development over the last ten years is a mistake. And so at both the popular level and the policy level there is something new about the debate.

At the beginning of the pastoral letter, the bishops explain that they wrote it for basically the same two purposes for which Catholic moral teaching on warfare has always existed. These purposes from at least the time of Augustine have been: to help shape the conscience of each individual believer on moral questions about the use of force, and to help set the right terms of public policy debate over the morality of the use of force. Those two purposes—shaping the individual conscience, shaping the public dialogue—correspond roughly to the two levels of the public argument today.

At one level, the nuclear question is political. It is about the policy of states, the public opinion of societies, and how states relate to one another in the nuclear age. The bishops did not seek to write a political document, however. They make it clear that at the heart of the political issue is a significant moral issue.

Thirty years ago, Romano Guardini, in a book called *Power of Responsibility*, argued that the key moral question for the rest of the century was whether we could develop the moral capacity to control the power we had already created. The point is interesting whether one is concerned about medical ethics or nuclear ethics. When we are able to do almost anything, how do we decide what we ought to do and what we ought never to do?

The political argument, given its usual limitations, has not raised this twofold question; it tends to move along the line of the technological drive. To introduce the moral question is to help reshape the public argument.

The pastoral letter tries to move beyond that. It says that a political issue that becomes a moral issue may also be described as a religious issue. It is religious in this sense, that when one looks at the stakes of the moral question, one begins to reach for the language usually reserved for religious discourse.

When the Pope went to Hiroshima he said, standing in front of the monument, "In the past, it was possible to destroy a town, a village, a region, even a nation—today it is the whole planet that is under threat, and the response of the human community must be a moral about-face." The pastoral letter argues that when the whole planet is, in principle, under threat, that is something more than a purely political issue.

The Basic Moral Premise

The formal object of the letter was to perform a moral and religious analysis of a political, strategic, and technical question.

The document's moral premise is one that has been central to Catholic moral teaching on warfare since at least the fourth century, the doctrine of a just or a limited war. According to this, some but not all uses of force are morally legitimate. This doctrine is faced with a revolutionary challenge in the nuclear age.

The pastoral letter asks in its third section, How do you *build* the peace in an increasingly interdependent world? This section deals with non-nuclear aspects of foreign policy.

The question that has attracted the most attention is dealt with in the second part. How do you *keep* the peace in the nuclear age? The bishops put forth both a strategic and a political argument. Their strategic argument proceeds in three steps: (1) a premise is set forth that (2) is related to three cases of use of nuclear weapons and (3) is then related to the strategy of deterrence.

The premise is that nuclear weapons constitute a qualitatively new challenge to the traditional moral arguments. The use of these weapons is not to be seen simply as a linear extension of past uses of force. The qualitatively new challenge concerns controllability. The tradition says that some uses of force are morally acceptable, but not all. The principle that any legitimate use of force must be a limited use is therefore central to the argument.

I describe this as part of the bishops' premise, though it is not a point they can define with the exactitude that they can have in some other areas of doctrine. The bishops are radically skeptical about the ability to control not just one use of the weapon but further use, and to bring that use to an end. On this question of the controllability of nuclear weapons I think the bishops may best be described as agnostic.

Categories of Use

Their doubts are pervasive when they address three potential kinds of use of nuclear weapons. The first is *directly intended attacks on civilians*. Such attacks, in Catholic moral theology, are always wrong. There are no exceptions. The principle is binding on all Catholics, and as the bishops' letter says, any Catholic asked to take part in such attacks is expected to refuse to obey orders. So binding is this rule, they go on to say, that directly intended attacks on civilian populations are not justified even if our own civilian population is hit first.

The next type of use is the so-called *first use*. Here the nature of the argument is different. In this case the bishops come to a moral conclusion, which is a mixture of moral principles with political, strategic, and technological considerations.

In the bishops' view, there is no case where first use of nuclear weapons can be justified, and so they argue against any first use. They acknowledge, however, that because this is a moral conclusion—a mixture of principle and fact—there is room for dissent and further discussion in the church.

The third case is what is called *limited nuclear war*. Here the bishops look at our ability to contain and control nuclear conflict within some recognizable moral bounds.

Once again, since it is not the kind of issue one can settle definitively, a radical skepticism runs through the argument. As the bishops put it after examining different positions on the issue, the burden of moral proof rests upon those who say the weapons can be used within a morally definable framework.

The Bishops and Deterrence

By the end of the section on use, what is left? The bishops have ruled out any use against civilian populations. They have ruled out, on the basis of prudential judgment, first use. They have expressed radical skepticism about limited use. But have they said that *any* use of a nuclear weapon under *any* circumstances in *any* way is intrinsically evil? No. They left a centimeter of ambiguity about use. And on that centimeter they hang the argument of deterrence.

They describe their position on deterrence as *strictly conditioned moral acceptance*. Each word carries some weight. It is acceptance rather than condemnation, but it is not pure acceptance.

"Strictly conditioned" as the bishops use it has two characteristics. The first is temporal: they argue that deterrence should be used as a framework to move from where we are to something different. Second, "strictly conditioned" describes the character of the deterrent. If the moral justification of the deterrent is to prevent the use of nuclear weapons under any circumstances, then the character of the deterrent needs to be shaped in such a way that its possessors are always seeking to limit the possibility that it will ever be used.

The political context of nuclear weapons, say the bishops, is a divided world. It is divided, first, into more than 160 nation states, all of which assume the right to use force, if necessary, and six of which have nuclear weapons. Second, the world is divided into two major systems dominated by two nuclear superpowers. The document argues that these states are divided from each other by philosophy, history, and ideology, that there really are differences between them, in moral values as well as in political ideology. But the document also says that the two have a definable common interest, which is that the use of these weapons will simply not be helpful politically or morally to either of them. On the basis of that common interest, the letter argues for a whole series of measures to contain, control, and reduce the significance of nuclear weapons.

The bishops are not unaware of the political uses of nuclear weapons. They therefore seek to reduce the ways in which states would try to gain political advantage from the nuclear threat, and thus to reduce that threat. The letter then goes on to discuss a whole series of arms-control measures.

During the forty years of the nuclear debate, there have been key moments when concepts became fluid, when ideas that previously had been accepted almost without question came under challenge. In such a fluid situation, certain concepts move in to crystallize the discussion and shape the debate. The late fifties was such a period. I think that we are in another of those open moments in the strategic debate, and that the possibility of redefining some aspects is very high.

The purpose of the pastoral letter is to contribute to that process.

The U.S. Catholic Bishops and Soviet Reality

MICHAEL NOVAK

At one time there was no comparison between the strength of the USSR and your own. Then it became equal to yours. Now as all recognize, it is becoming superior to yours. Perhaps today the ratio is just greater than equal, but soon it will be two to one. Then three to one. Finally it will be five to one. . . . With such nuclear superiority it will be possible to block the use of your weapons, and on some unlucky morning they will declare: "Attention. We are sending our troops into Europe, and if you make a move we will annihilate you." And this ratio of three to one or five to one will have its effect: you will not make a move.
          —ALEKSANDR SOLZHENITSYN[1]

U NLIKE SOLZHENITSYN, the U.S. Catholic bishops do not urge the West to rearm itself to meet the present danger. They throw their weight, instead, on the side of those who counsel disarmament. At a moment of maximum danger, their 1983 Pastoral Letter on War and Peace counseled the ways of good will, negotiations, and trust. History alone will show whether what they said was an act of moral illumination, as some judge, or of moral obscurantism and appeasement, as others judge. Final judgment will depend disproportionately on the deeds of the Soviet Union.

Throughout their letter, the bishops seem to assume that the threat of nuclear war emanates most from American actions. Yet the Soviet Union has a doctrine that imposes on its loyal believers an obligation to make socialism triumph universally. Russian traditions of imperial prerogative gain strength from the Soviet viewpoint that socialism is the tide of history, the Soviet state its vanguard, the Red Army its sword.

Michael Novak holds the George Frederick Jewett Chair for Public Policy Research at the American Enterprise Institute, Washington, D.C. Among his books are *The Spirit of Democratic Capitalism* and *Confession of a Catholic*. This essay, previously published in the November/December 1983 issue of *New Catholic World* and used by permission, parallels his address at the seminars from which the other essays in the book were drawn.

SHIFT IN THE BALANCE OF FORCES

Three fundamental changes in the balance of forces between the U.S.S.R. and the United States during the past ten years seem to confirm the Soviet vision. (1) After the Cuban missile crisis, Soviet *strategic* nuclear forces made such dramatic leaps forward that they were said to be at "rough parity" with American strategic forces by the time of the SALT I agreements of 1972. Since then, they have leapt forward again to several forms of superiority. (2) Soviet *theater* nuclear weapons have placed European cities under the threat of almost instant annihilation through the SS-20s. (3) Soviet *conventional* forces have reached virtual qualitative parity with Western conventional forces while continuing to hold enormous advantages in quantities of troops, tanks, aircraft, and artillery pieces.[2]

The decade of the eighties can be seen, then, as a time of clear and present danger for the United States, a period during which the correlation of forces is temporarily in favor of the Soviet Union to a degree never reached before nor likely to be reached again, once America has rearmed itself.

If one looks at the planet strategically, observing the key pressure points, one also sees that Soviet assets have grown steadily. The Soviet navy now maintains fleets in the South China Sea (with bases in Vietnam), in the Indian Ocean, and in the Mediterranean Sea, where Western shipping was earlier unchallenged. Moreover, the Soviets maintain armed nuclear submarines near both coasts of the United States and in the Caribbean (with bases in Cuba). The Soviet capacity to cut Africa off from America in the South Atlantic is also growing steadily. Finally, Soviet air and naval power in the North Atlantic can no longer be halted by U.S. forces in Iceland and Greenland.

What the Bishops Don't Say

But the bishops pay scant attention to the changed quantity and quality, location and activities, of Soviet armed power. In calling for "an end to the arms race," the bishops do not assess the present balance of power or the recent shift in it. They judge that peace will become more likely if the United States cuts back military spending and continues on its decline relative to Soviet power. They mention no "present danger" from Soviet arms growth.

The advance of Soviet military power may one day awaken the American public as never before. At that point, even the bishops will discover how weak, relative to Soviet military power, the United States has become. The Soviets now have both the strategic potential, which they never had before, and the structural proclivities, of which over the years they have given ample evidence, to expand their military control over any one of many new targets of opportunity.

There is already an active legion of East German, Bulgarian, Czech, Russian, Cuban, Libyan, and PLO combatants in Central America. It is not difficult to imagine that Iran and Iraq could join Afghanistan by 1990 as forward bases for Soviet aircraft, intelligence units, and rapid deployment forces. With adroit boldness, Soviet leadership might also renegotiate the borders of Poland and East Germany, expanding East German control over the poorly performing industrial cities of western Poland. Simultaneously, without formal reunification, West and East Germany would be pressured to sign pacts committing both to "disarmament" and "neutralization." Soviet military power would ensure the Finlandization of the strongest nation in continental Western Europe.

Moreover, a rising genius in the Soviet military might well argue that the worldwide "correlation of forces" is more in favor of the USSR than it has ever been, or is likely to be in the future, and that before the current weapons systems become obsolete they ought to be used to ensure Soviet security for generations to come.

Two Possible Scenarios

The strategic calculations would run as follows. No U.S. leader would commit American cities to destruction in order to defend Europe. The Soviets could, therefore, force Western Europe to capitulate in one of two ways. The most daring way would be to destroy one European city—perhaps Hamburg—with a sudden rain of SS-20s. According to the U.S. bishops, no nuclear retaliation by the West would be morally permissible; in any case, no retaliation would be likely. Citizens in the United States would be loathe to have the scenes from Hamburg, witnessed on television, repeated in, say, Minneapolis—St. Paul. The Soviets would offer a non-aggression pact, holding Soviet troops out of Western Europe. All they would ask in exchange would be European disarmament.

In Europe, many on the left already champion European neutralism. Political pressure in this direction would be strengthened by the overwhelming military power of the Soviet Union, poised for further destruction.

Once Europe had preemptively surrendered in the largest matter, many smaller surrenders would be demanded. Anti-Soviet publications would be considered violations of neutrality. Broadcasting services to Eastern Europe—the Vatican, the BBC, Radio Free Europe—would be banned. Anything violating Soviet sovereignty and privilege would be punished. Leaders from European Communist parties would be favored as the most appropriate representatives to send to Moscow for the conduct of trade and other matters. Assassinations of independent-minded leaders would routinely occur and routinely be "deplored" by Moscow. American companies in Europe would be nationalized if possible, or expelled. Anti-American propaganda would gain intensity. Use of the European media would be restricted to friends of "peace, neutrality, and solidarity."

This is one scenario. Another is more brutal. Intent on demonstrating that the Red Army is invincible, the Soviet general staff would unleash its full fury on the north German plain, warning that resort to tactical nuclear weapons by NATO would be met by the swift destruction of one city after another by SS-20s. Following Soviet battle doctrine, the Red Army would strike in massed formations, wave after wave, breaking through thin NATO defenses at will in three selected corridors, aiming to reach the Rhine within three weeks.

Fleeing refugees in millions of automobiles would clog every highway, making effective reinforcement of military posts impossible. Modern cities being easier than ancient cities to paralyze, thousands of intelligence officers now under deep cover in West Germany would move to assigned assaults upon communications and information systems. Almost as swiftly as General Jaruzelski broke the back of Solidarity—i.e., in a single night—West Germany would be stricken. The negotiated nonaggression pact would provide that all American forces humbly disembark within thirty days.

The lesson to the world would be stark. If NATO could not resist the Red Army, could Pakistan, Iran, or Saudi Arabia? Could Israel? Concessions from everywhere would flow toward Moscow.

The Catholic bishops may have read the "signs of the times" correctly, but history may judge them guilty of immense miscalculations. Talking of peace is a proven Leninist tactic. When the Soviets prepare for war (as in Afghanistan), they invariably launch a "peace offensive." Talking of peace is cheap, and it easily feeds illusions and complacence.

Toward 'Progressive Disarmament'

In the face of the unprecedented buildup of Soviet military power, the bishops place great faith in negotiations. They recommend a halt to the further deployment and testing of nuclear weapons. They urge negotiated deep cuts in the nuclear arsenals of both sides. And they call for an "early and successful conclusion of negotiations of a comprehensive test ban treaty."

These recommendations derive from the bishops' general principle: "Nuclear deterrence should be used as a step on the way toward progressive disarmament." "Progressive" sounds odd here. Can the bishops possibly mean "progressive" in the generic sense of "socialist"? They cannot mean *unilateral* disarmament, which they say they are against. So they must mean *negotiated* disarmament. But far from being "progressive," disarmament efforts during the last century or so have been extremely disheartening. Consider the judgment cited by Barbara Tuchman:

> The trouble with disarmament was (and still is) that the problem of war is tackled upside down and at the wrong end. . . . Nations don't distrust each other because they are armed; they are armed because they distrust each other. And therefore to want disarmament before a minimum of common agreement on fundamentals is as absurd as to want people to go undressed in winter.[3]

Even political commentator Theodore Draper, writing in the *New York Review of Books,* is not very encouraging:

Once different weapons and even different weapons systems must be evaluated and balanced off against each other, negotiations inevitably degenerate into endlessly futile haggling sessions, brought to a close only by agreement on a crazy quilt of trade-offs and loopholes. Negotiations of this sort become more important for the mere consolation that the deadly antagonists are negotiating than for anything the negotiations may bring forth. . . . Short of abolishing all nuclear weapons forever and everywhere, deterrence is all we have.[4]

Has disarmament been "progressive" since the Napoleonic wars? Since the Civil War, or 1914, or 1945? Has the Soviet Union ever disarmed in any respect whatever? After 1968, Defense Secretary McNamara expected that a virtual U.S. nuclear freeze would enable the Soviet Union to come up to parity and halt. It did not halt.

Historians can point to two major examples of "progressive disarmament"—apart from the enforced disarming of West Germany and Japan following World War II. Both were conducted by the United States. The first was the demobilization of U.S. forces in Europe within eighteen months of the cessation of hostilities, which Roosevelt rashly promised the unbelieving Stalin at Yalta. The second was the relative nuclear disarmament of the United States after 1968, under McNamara's illusion that the Soviets would reach parity with us and stop. Congress after Congress was elected in the 1970s to "cut the defense budget." Indeed, the U.S. budget for defense went down by 19 per cent in constant 1983 dollars between 1970 and 1981—from $223 billion to $183 billion.[5] Since 1968 the number of U.S. land-based missile-launchers has remained constant at 1,054. Strategic bombers have decreased by attrition from 1,364 in 1964 to 272 in 1983. The nuclear warheads in the U.S. arsenal have been reduced in number and size, and the total throw-weight of all our missiles has been reduced by more than half.[6]

The bishops do not, however, praise the United States for such "progressive disarmament." To do so would call attention to the feverish and herculean efforts of the USSR to achieve something far beyond nuclear parity (which was publicly declared to exist in 1972): both nuclear and conventional superiority in every field. Here the bishops enter the field of moral wistfulness. They write: "We must continually say no to the idea of nuclear war." Such words are not like the words of transubstantiation; saying them does not change reality. Nor will "progressive disarmament" occur because the bishops need it in order to justify, by their lights, moral reliance on deterrence. Deterrence is morally obligatory *whether or not* "progressive disarmament" leaps from the world of myth into the world of fact—and will be even more necessary if it does not.

The bishops assume that the Soviet leaders *will* disarmament. This is a fundamental misunderstanding. Neither Marxist ideology about the moral obligation to use force nor the practice of the Soviets since 1917 gives any empirical support to such an assumption. When the United States reduced its nuclear forces, the USSR could have caught up and rested; it caught up and did not rest. The Soviet Union wills to negotiate nothing except the permanent inferiority of the United States, and a consequent pattern of subservience to the "laws of history." This cannot be negotiated in justice.

JUSTICE IN NEGOTIATIONS

Although the world has long had a moral theory about justice in war, it has no classical statement of moral guidance for justice in negotiations. Not all negotiations are morally just. Some negotiations succeed through intimidation, some through cowardice. The ill and dying Roosevelt at Yalta was rude toward Churchill, fawning toward Stalin, and catastrophically unjust to the peoples of Eastern Europe.[7] These same peoples had already suffered more than their share through an earlier unjust negotiation, the Molotov-Ribbentrop Pact. Some believe the Helsinki Accords added to the injustice, in as yet unmeasured ways. Whatever the moral status of particular cases, it seems obvious that negotiations between great powers cannot escape moral scrutiny. The Catholic bishops have given thought to the morality of warfare, but very little to the calculus of moral evils involved inevitably in every negotiation aimed at peace.

Two more examples bear on the point. The "unconditional surrender" imposed by the Allies on Germany after World War II was not clearly an act of moral justice. Neither were the negotiations at Versailles at the end of World War I.

In all negotiation, the weaker party may be obliged to accept injustice. One cannot, therefore, as the bishops do, simply judge deterrence by the outcome of negotiations. Rather, one must judge the outcome of negotiations by the power of deterrence. Factors of power are of elementary importance.

Further, the asymmetry between democratic states and totalitarian states ipso facto injures the moral standing of negotiations. Democratic peoples reach consensus through public contests, and therefore typically negotiate first against themselves; totalitarian powers wait and watch. (They also penetrate domestic debates within open societies.)

Power in totalitarian states rests in the will of a collective few, insulated from public discussion, operating in secrecy, and bound by no standard but their own national aggrandizement. In democratic states, one government is not always like another; public consensus shifts; moral standards and public laws have enormous public power, even compelling presidential resignations. It is difficult, therefore, to imagine wholly moral and just relations between democratic and totalitarian states. Agreements between them can only be codified statements of existing correlations of force and national interest.

Differing Aims

Finally, the aim of negotiations, once entered into, is quite different for democratic and for totalitarian powers. Totalitarian states have no need to reach an agreement. They can be sublimely indifferent. They can concentrate every energy upon one sole aim: increasing their power by every possible means. For their legitimacy flows not from the esteem of others but from their own tightly clenched power.

By contrast, once democratic powers enter into negotiations, their leaders are quickly held accountable to standards of universal reason and moral principle. To come home with "nothing" is for them, but not for totalitarian leaders, a public failure. Consequently, it is relatively easy for totalitarian masters of the dynamics of negotiations to concentrate attention upon cosmetic concessions whose words are meaningful only within free, open, and moral societies, and have no substance whatever within regimes based upon lies. Furthermore, Western negotiators typically want agreements that are simple, clear, and easy to "verify." They define weapons systems and other military matters in this light, which is often a false light.[8]

In a word, negotiations between a totalitarian and a democratic power can never be like negotiations between partners who share a similar moral vision, intellectual tradition, and common meanings. The language of such negotiations is, inevitably, like Alice in Wonderland. Typically, too, serious issues are relegated to unsigned appendices and memorandums of understanding, with a proviso that all parties understand them according to their own laws, institutions, customs, and authorities.

From these plain facts, a strong case can be made that any negotiation with a totalitarian power is almost certainly unjust; if just, it is so only by accident, as it suits the totalitarian power. Parchment barriers do not constrain those whose power comes from no parchment.

A Parody of Christian Morality

"Progressive disarmament" is a phrase uttered by those who despair of the real-world competition of military power. Giving up that struggle, they plead with the stronger power to do likewise. Whatever else it is, this plea is not Christian morality, only a parody thereof.

While negotiations with the Soviets must, for various reasons, go on, they can be only as effective as the military power that bends Soviet will. What Soviet morality compels Soviet will to desire in the absence of constraining force is shown in more than six decades of bloody history. Since 1923, according to Solzhenitsyn,[9] Soviet authorities have put 65 million of their own citizens to death for political reasons; they have also subjugated some thirty-one nations.

Indeed, one has only to alter the subject of "progressive disarmament" from "Soviets" to "Nazis" to see the absurdity of identifying religious hope with confidence in the reasonable mercies of totalitarian leaders.

The net geopolitical impact of the bishops' letter was to contribute to illusions. The bishops did resist pacifism; that is to their credit. They did not, despite much activism, deny the morality of deterrence; that, too, is to their credit. But they failed to promote the clarity of soul necessary to make deterrence work, and that flaw injures their pastoral letter both as a religious and as a political document. By contrast, the pastoral letter of the bishops of France was more deeply rooted in Christian realism.

Nuclear Pacifism and True Peace

FRANS A. M. ALTING VON GEUSAU

FOR THE THIRD TIME since the end of the Second World War, pacifism—that is, nuclear pacifism—has appeared on the Western political scene. In the few years since 1977, the so-called peace movements have grown into an intricate and vociferous international network and a strange "alternative" political subculture. Two principal strands should be immediately distinguished in this network: (1) the "useful" or *Soviet-manipulated pacifists*, loyally promoting Soviet "peace" campaigns through a vast network of Communist front organizations, who are manipulated by the Communist Party of the Soviet Union, especially its International Department; and (2) the *virtuous pacifists*, involved in what they call autonomous peace movements, who are products of an unreasoning fear of nuclear war and a feeling of impotence about the ongoing arms race.

Pacifists of the first type carry out instructions for Soviet political warfare aimed at the strategic defeat of the West. All I shall say about them here is that they cooperate closely with the virtuous pacifists in Western Europe, whose message I shall examine.

Pacifists, and many church leaders in their wake, appear to consider peace the highest value, if not an absolute one, in relations between sovereign states in the nuclear age. But what they mean by peace is yet to be defined.

Frans A. M. Alting von Geusau is professor of the law of international and European organizations at the Catholic University of Tilburg, the Netherlands, and director of the John F. Kennedy Institute Center for International Studies. He is the chairman of the Advisory Commission on Disarmament and International Security to the Dutch government.

True and False Peace

Peace is the object of a profound human desire and evokes only positive emotions. Unless peace is defined, however, the longing for it can easily be abused. It has been systematically abused by the Soviet Communist party since 1917. In the words of Lenin: "As an ultimate objective, peace simply means Communist world control." Soviet "peace" campaigns are meant to weaken and defeat the United States and Western Europe. The peace they promote is nothing else than servitude, or a false peace without God.

Even those virtuous pacifists who openly dissociate themselves from this false peace—and they are not many—hold an undefined, vague, and not very Christian notion of peace. They tend to construct a continuum from *peace in the hearts of men*, through *peace and trust among people*, to *peace among peoples and states*. According to them, only military-industrial complexes, military alliances, deterrence systems, security elites, and the like stand in the way of trust and peace among peoples. Such a view is not only a dangerous illusion and a philosophical error; it is also an insult to the oppressed people in totalitarian states. The pacifists' principal philosophical error lies in blindness to the essential difference between peaceful relations among men in an organized society, and peaceful relations among sovereign states.

In an organized society, justice will bring about peace. However, justice requires a legal order and a political authority to uphold and, if necessary, enforce it. In relations among states, neither a proper legal order nor an adequate political authority exists. Therefore a balance of power must be maintained to uphold justice.

The Czechoslovak citizens in the human-rights movement called Charter 77[1] wrote in 1977: "Experience has taught us that respect for the rights and freedoms of its own citizens is a criterion of the sincerity of any government's peace effort." Vladimir Bukovsky expressed the same thought: "The two sides of the Soviet regime— internal oppression and external aggressiveness—are inseparably interlocked, creating a sort of vicious circle."

Peace should be seen as the fruit of justice; in the absence of justice, the pacifist notion of peace is an escape from reality. A crucial Christian insight is that evil, cruelty, and sin are a part of reality. In the world of man, full justice will be forever unattainable. Therefore the use of force to maintain or promote human justice cannot be eliminated from this world.

The Context of Peace

Democratic governments have a duty to stand for the values of liberty, justice, and human dignity, as well as peace. To treat the desire for peace in isolation from these other values is to advocate the view that nothing is more important than personal or collective survival. The consequences of such a position are that civic courage loses its character as a virtue, and freedom, justice, and human dignity lose their character as values. Such a moral stance disguises an attitude composed of unreasoning fear, a longing for tranquility, a desire to escape from responsibility for dealing with the real world, and submissiveness to superior force.

Today's pacifists are *nuclear pacifists*. In their desire for peace, they do not reject the use of force altogether, but only its riskier forms. Nuclear pacifists declare nuclear weapons to be the greatest moral issue of our time. It is a sign of the current moral and spiritual crisis that certain instruments for deterrence and defense, rather than the perpetrators of evil and war among men, are seen as the greatest moral issue. It is a sign of confusion, moreover, that symptoms of a world in conflict—arms and arms buildups—are treated as the causes of war.

Such an argument also reflects a neglect of the political context in which arms are developed, and a shocking moral indifference toward the distinction between the character and intentions of democratic governments and of totalitarian regimes. The apparent impartiality of the pacifists in this respect unavoidably slides into dishonesty when, for instance, one compares their vicious attacks on the U.S. government with their unfounded "understanding" of Kremlin behavior, or when one sees their neglect of human rights issues, such as those presented by Charter 77.

The New Political Subculture

Nuclear pacifists today belong to what I view as an alternative political subculture. In it, activists of many divergent persuasions are held together by a climate of unreasoning fear, and their consequent actions are justified by irrational slogans. Simplified notions of "the arms race," deterrence systems, military blocs, and so on serve to disguise and distort political realities that the pacifists refuse even to examine. Their appeal to the emotions of the masses prevents rational debate. Their experts manipulate data. They speak their own language and willfully reject the majority political culture of democratic discussion, decision-making, and the rule of law. Focusing their attention on fighting specific Western nuclear weapons programs, they are able to combine the agitation of groups as far apart as concerned middle-of-the-road Christian Democrats and Soviet-controlled front organizations. Their message appears to be that the strategy of deterrence either is wrong per se or will not prevent a war forever.

Some pacifists advocate unilateral moves toward nuclear disarmament on the basis of a totally unfounded belief that the Soviet leadership would then react with disarmament moves of its own. Others advocate unilateral disarmament because they believe they can choose life under Soviet domination over death in a nuclear war. They fail to understand that "red or dead" is not an alternative but a sequence. The real alternative we face is not peace *versus* war but freedom and life *versus* slavery and death. Still other pacifists, like the Ground Zero group in the United States, call for a "new strategy" to deal with the Soviet Union. They fail to recognize that the totalitarian nature of the Soviet regime is a reality that we must face rather than some misperception that we can change. Ground Zero's approach apparently derives from the frivolous, abstract theory that international relations is a zero-sum game, one in which a gain on one side involves a loss on the other.

The components of this subculture have, as a common denominator, a refusal of the moral duty to consider the consequences of their proposals and agitation. In their wake, a rising chorus of church leaders has come forward with premature and ill-founded moral pronouncements on such political issues as "no first use," the threat of use of nuclear weapons, and the "inadmissibility" of certain strategic doctrines. By their moral pronouncements, these church leaders raise the level of fear and popular emotionalism but do not convince responsible governments to dismantle the principal means of deterrence and defense against aggression. They thus contribute to intolerance, disagreement, and political distrust in our societies, and ultimately to increased chances of war.

Whoever fails to examine the issue of the costs of deterrence and defense *versus* the costs of war and totalitarian repression, whoever fails to recognize that a no-first-use policy or a freeze will be the beginning of the end of NATO and will expose Western Europe to Soviet nuclear blackmail and domination, has no right to make moral pronouncements. The message of these church leaders is a disservice to democratic society, to human dignity, and to the cause of peace.

THE PROBLEM OF POWER

Even in the nuclear era, the fundamental ethical problem in national and international politics is the problem of power over men: its use, its restraints, and its legitimacy.

The first duty of political authority is to create and uphold a legal order in which justice, liberty, and human dignity prevail. Legal order and the rule of law require a competent political authority to uphold and if necessary enforce them. This requirement reflects the profound human reality of inequity and conflict. Why is it that so many church leaders who are eager to teach about nuclear weapons have failed to address themselves to this fundamental ethical dilemma of power over men?

Governments, like societies, are composed not of saints or detached philosophers but of fallen men and women subject to the drive or instinct of power—mastery—and the accompanying abuse of power. We may hope that our political leaders are imbued with the virtues of meekness, prudence, and restraint. Reality teaches us, however, that the power exercised by human beings must be restrained and checked by countervailing power. Such a system of checks and balances has been achieved in the Western democracies. In the totalitarian one-party states of our century, we have seen the exercise of unrestrained power produce not virtue and justice but oppression, terror, and the unrestrained *abuse* of power.

The inherent dynamics of totalitarian oppression and expansion confront the Western democracies with the choice between resisting further totalitarian expansion, with force if necessary, and exposing their citizens to this kind of oppression. Western governments are morally obliged to choose resistance. The policies they conduct and the instruments they use may not be judged good or bad in purely abstract terms. In each situation, they must be judged in concrete terms to determine whether they are more or less morally acceptable than the alternatives.

CONDITIONS FOR PEACE IN TODAY'S WORLD

Opposition to the theory of just war and the view that nuclear war is morally inadmissible have, in my opinion, focused attention on the wrong issues. The opposition is mainly a creation of the pacifists, who discuss only *war-fighting* scenarios while neglecting the major strategic problem facing the Western alliance, namely, the continuing buildup of a Soviet military capability.

The primary Western problem is to develop a morally acceptable *war-prevention* theory. This theory must examine the acceptability of the strategy of deterrence as a means, possibly in conjunction with others, of preventing aggression and war. Such a theory must try to indicate the moral obligations in dealing with particular situations.

The international situation we are in today is, first of all, one made up of sovereign states that do not recognize any higher political authority. Power rather than the rule of law prevails in their mutual relations. Western democracies, whose governments have a duty to protect their citizens against war and aggression, must therefore carefully assess any threat to their security. In the nuclear era and in the particular situation of East-West division in Europe, Western democracies are confronted with a threat—emerging from Soviet "total foreign policy"[2]—to human dignity plus the threat of a nuclear attack. This means the possibility of a more awesome total war than the world has experienced in this century.

The Right of Self-Defense

The charter of the United Nations was designed at the end of the Second World War to be the principal instrument for preventing war. It prohibited the use of force in the pursuit of national interests and offered alternative peaceful means for settling conflicts among states. If such settlement failed, the Security Council could take enforcement measures against breaches of the peace or acts of aggression. Provisions for the regulation of armaments were to be implemented to complete a system maintaining international peace and security. The charter recognized the states' inherent right to individual and collective self-defense against an armed attack if the U.N. security system were to fail. It *has* failed in East-West relations, and collective arrangements for self-defense have become the cornerstone of Western defense and security policies.

A strategy of *deterrence* has become the instrument both to prevent war and to control warfare if deterrence should fail. The argument that the strategy may be fallible or cannot forever prevent war is not very pertinent to the particular situation confronting the West. Deterrence strategy has so far served the West against the Soviet Union. It can be replaced by another strategy only if the replacement is demonstrably better able to prevent war. Thus far, pacifists and Ground Zero-style thinkers have only produced proposals that would make war more likely, given the existing international situation.

Only *negotiations* offer hope for multilateral and verifiable reductions in arms and for reducing the likelihood of war. It is a moral duty for governments in the present situation to create better conditions for more successful negotiations. The first such condition is the existence of mutual interest in achieving progress. Such interest, on the part of the Soviet Union, will emerge only when the Kremlin knows that unilateral gains through military superiority or political warfare are no longer within reach.

The Principal Western Duty

To achieve positive conditions for negotiation, the West must redress the military imbalance, but above all it must restore its own political solidarity. The restoration of confidence among the allies and of internal political consensus in NATO member states is, indeed, the principal moral and political duty of Western governments. This duty cannot be discharged unless our common belief in our own democratic values is revived and unless governments and peoples are willing to sustain these values.

The strength of the alliance ultimately depends upon the moral strength of the allied societies. The moral and spiritual crisis in many Western states is the most worrisome source of weakness against the Soviet totalitarian threat. It is this weakness to which Aleksandr Solzhenitsyn referred some years ago in his Harvard commencement speech:

> We, the oppressed people of Russia, the oppressed peoples of Eastern Europe, watch with anguish the tragic enfeeblement of Europe. We offer you the experience of our suffering; we would like you to accept it without having to pay the monstrous price of death and slavery that we have paid.

If the West fails to heed his warning, future historians may have to write of us as an ancient historian once wrote of the Athenians:

> In the end, more than they wanted freedom, they wanted security. They wanted a comfortable life and they lost it all— security, comfort, and freedom. . . . When the Athenians finally wanted not to give to society but for society to give to them, when the freedom they wished for most was freedom from responsibility, then Athens ceased to be free.

The Western democracies are not yet condemned to go down the same road as the Athenians. With much more chance of success than the oppressed peoples of Russia and Eastern Europe—the West's strongest allies—we can and must resist totalitarian oppression and expansion. It needs only a fraction of the civic courage and moral fortitude expressed by the Polish workers who inscribed on the cross erected before the Lenin Shipyard in Gdansk the final passage of Psalm 29:

> *May the Lord give strength to His people!*
> *May the Lord bless His people with peace!*

NATO and 'First Use'

ROBERT A. GESSERT

S INCE 1945 EUROPE has enjoyed the longest period of peace within recent history. It is not coincidental that there have been nuclear weapons on both sides of that divided continent.

I do not like nuclear weapons, and I do not like heavy dependence on nuclear weapons, but I don't see how they can be eliminated. I think it is a disservice for U.S. presidents, Catholic bishops, or anyone else to create the illusion that nuclear weapons will ever be eliminated from the face of the earth, let alone in a foreseeable future. Even if they were all eliminated, they would be created again. Our problem is to learn how to live with their reality—to use their existence as an effective deterrent to aggression, and to develop well-conceived capabilities and plans for their use to end an aggression if deterrence should fail. In peacetime, we must do all we can to make sure that we have some rational, *controlled* use of nuclear weapons in mind in case we are ever forced to use them.

I agree emphatically with the Catholic bishops in condemning any doctrine that says nuclear weapons should be used principally against population centers. Intentional destruction of cities even in retaliation is a morally inadmissible use of nuclear weapons. I hold this judgment primarily on ethical grounds, but I also believe that such destruction makes no sense politically and strategically. Retaliation should be aimed at military targets.

That either superpower would attempt a preemptive first strike against the other seems highly unlikely. The fear of a surprise attack, or of a massive use of nuclear weapons in the first exchange, seems likewise unrealistic. I disagreed with the distinguished members of

Robert A. Gessert is a research fellow of the Logistics Management Institute, Washington, D.C., and the author of more than twenty studies of national security for the U.S. government. He is an ordained minister of the United Church of Christ and is co-chairman of the International Council on Christian Approaches to Defense and Disarmament.

the Committee on the Present Danger[1] who, at the end of the 1970s, identified a "window of vulnerability," suggesting that sometime in the mid-eighties the Soviet Union might contemplate a first strike against the continental United States. That possibility is so remote that it should have little influence on our strategic planning.

More significant is the danger of getting into nuclear war by escalation, by accident, by a terrorist's use of nuclear weapons, or by the action of some new nuclear power that has not learned the responsibilities of possessing nuclear weapons.

ERRORS IN DETERRENCE THEORY

A lot of our discussion of deterrence has an Alice in Wonderland quality. Somewhere along the line, our theory went astray. In my view, this point was the Cuban missile crisis of 1962. In President Kennedy's speech demanding the removal of the Soviet missiles from Cuba, he said in effect that one missile landing anywhere in the Western Hemisphere, fired from the island of Cuba, would be sufficient to warrant the release of the total strategic retaliatory capability of the United States against the Soviet Union. That's an astonishing statement. Such a response would be a flagrant violation of the just war doctrine and its principles of discrimination and proportionality. But most people have judged this U.S. threat by its apparent success in ending the crisis.

Since then we have tended to believe that deterrence rests on that kind of overstatement of what our response would be to any kind of aggression. The principle seems to be that the more we overstate it, the more irrational we make our response appear, the more it exceeds the limits of discrimination and proportionality, the better it is as a deterrent. I say, nonsense!

The resort to overstatement—or irrationality—has poisoned the discussion of deterrence theory. From it stemmed all the arguments that anything we did to create the possibility of a controlled, rational use of nuclear weapons weakened deterrence. That is true only if our notion of deterrence is the bizarre one that was involved in the Cuban missile crisis.

There is another error in our thinking about deterrence. We talk as though it were directed at some abstract thing, or some inanimate thing, called "war." But what we are actually trying to deter is a potential *aggressor* or aggressor state.

We want to deter an opponent from some contemplated act of aggression. We also want to prevent war. But these two objectives are not identical, and in some circumstances they may not even be compatible. In order to deter an aggressor, we may need to be willing to risk or to undertake war.

We are trying to *prevent war* insofar as possible, but first and foremost we are trying to *deter aggression* by means of our military capabilities. Therefore our failure to deter the aggressor from undertaking an attack does not mean that everything is over. It does not mean there is no longer any possibility of deterrence. Former Secretary of Defense James Schlesinger made this point in his annual report of January 1974, when he spoke of intra-war deterrence. The reason we need controlled, selective response options is to be able to continue deterrence during wartime. Why? To bring the aggression to an end, and to terminate war.

In contrast, former Secretary of Defense Robert McNamara has increasingly seemed to suggest in recent years that if war ever starts, deterrence has totally failed, and that there is nothing we can do in war to bring the war to an end. In an article in the Fall 1983 issue of *Foreign Affairs*,[2] he does acknowledge that the early attempts at flexible response had two aims: to prevent war and, if prevention failed, to bring war to an end. But he essentially repudiates that second purpose now.

McNamara now argues emphatically that the only use of nuclear weapons is to prevent war. If that use fails, then nuclear weapons have no more utility. He does not say what he wants to do with them in that event—whether he wants to surrender or destroy them. What he does say is that if they have not prevented war there is nothing else he can tell us. A responsible former secretary of defense should be able to tell us more than that.

NATO and First Use

We have created in NATO an alliance in which the superpower that has nuclear weapons has encouraged other members of the alliance, particularly the Federal Republic of Germany, to forswear the possession of nuclear weapons and to rest its security under the nuclear umbrella that we provide.

That worked fine, according to most contemporary commentators who now argue for a no-first-use doctrine, as long as the United States had a clear strategic nuclear superiority. It worked from the beginning of the alliance in 1949 probably throughout the sixties, although Mr. McNamara now says he wasn't so sure of that even in the early 1960s.

McNamara also states that he advised President Kennedy and President Johnson that under no circumstances should they ever be the first to use nuclear weapons. I'm not sure he was also telling our allies that, because they evidently believed that they would be shielded from a conventional attack by the probability, if not the certainty, that the United States would respond with nuclear weapons if necessary to stop such an attack. But the former secretary of defense now says he was telling our presidents something else in private conversations.

The Flexible Response Strategy

Of course, McNamara was trying to persuade our allies to adopt a strategy of flexible response, which he outlined in a ministerial meeting in Athens in 1962. The allies did in fact adopt the guidelines for that strategy proposed in 1962, but, as he also acknowledges, it took five more years of intense debate before NATO in 1967 formally adopted the strategy of flexible response (NATO Document MC-14/3, "Overall Strategic Concept for the Defense of the NATO Area").

According to the flexible response strategy as adopted in 1967, NATO has essentially three options for response to an attack. It could use any one of these three, or perhaps a mixture, depending on the nature of the attack: (1) "direct defense," which means a conventional defense against a limited conventional attack; (2) "deliberate escalation," which everyone understands to be a nuclear response to an overwhelming conventional attack and, therefore, the first use of nuclear weapons; and (3) "general nuclear response," which presumably would be the response to a nuclear attack and would invoke the United States' general nuclear release plan, SIOP (Single Integrated Operational Plan).

After much hard debate and negotiation, those became the three key elements of MC-14/3, the flexible response strategy. Evidently Mr. McNamara didn't really like the second element. He did argue long and hard for the first element, direct defense, and he now appears to regard that as essentially the only option NATO should have. (I think, by the way, that McNamara was better in the 1960s than he says he was, and I disagree with his reading of that history.)

Rejecting First Use

In a well-known article that appeared in the Spring 1982 issue of *Foreign Affairs*, McNamara and three other former high U.S. officials rejected the first use of nuclear weapons and urged that NATO announce a no-first-use pledge.[3] The other three were McGeorge Bundy, national security advisor to Presidents Kennedy and Johnson; George Kennan, former U.S. ambassador to Moscow; and Gerard Smith, chief negotiator for SALT I and former head of the U.S. Arms Control and Disarmament Agency.

In essence, their argument is very much like the one that President Charles de Gaulle had made quite a bit earlier against the strategy of flexible response: no U.S. president would ever be advised by his secretary of defense, or anyone else, to use strategic nuclear weapons against the Soviet Union in response to a conventional attack against Western Europe. To do so would be virtually suicidal, almost compelling a nuclear counterstrike against the United States.

This reasoning is not quite so self-serving on the part of the United States as it sounds, because, in the view of these four men, NATO's first use of nuclear weapons would be as suicidal for Western Europe as for the United States. In fact, it would probably be *more* so, because the first use itself might inflict severe damage on Western Europe if directed at attacking forces that had breached Western defenses. Moreover, Western Europe could scarcely be expected to be spared any counterstrikes. So it is hard, in their view, to see how Western Europe would be defended by NATO's using nuclear weapons first. Rather, it appears that, in the resultant escalation,

Western Europe along with much of the United States would be destroyed.

McNamara, Bundy, Kennan, and Smith tend to agree with the U.S. Catholic bishops that no controlled use of nuclear weapons is possible. Therefore nuclear weapons have no other utility than to prevent war by their mere existence. The first use of nuclear weapons in war would be suicidal.

The four Americans go on to say that the present position of implied first use detracts from NATO's willingness to build an adequate conventional defense capability. McNamara points out that, even though America's European allies accepted flexible response in principle, they never were willing to commit the resources to make direct (i.e., conventional) defense a viable option.

According to the four, the present first-use posture also invites war because the threat it presents to the other side is not credible. If first use is suicidal, as alleged, it would not be likely to be carried out even *in extremis*. If the first-use posture also detracts from building a conventional capability, it weakens resistance and deterrence across the full spectrum of possible attacks.

A European Response

Four German statesmen responded to the Americans' article in the succeeding issue of *Foreign Affairs*.[4] The four— Karl Kaiser, director of the Research Institute of the German Society for Foreign Affairs; Georg Leber, former Social Democratic minister of defense; Alois Mertes, a leading Christian Democratic foreign-policy spokesman; and General Franz-Josef Schulze, former commander-in-chief of Allied forces in Central Europe—argued that for NATO to adopt a no-first-use pledge would mark the beginning of the end of the alliance.

Their argument hinges on the assertion that the possibility, if not the certainty, of a U.S. first use in response to a conventional attack "couples" the U.S. strategic deterrent to the defense of Europe. The present first-use posture couples Europe and America, as it couples conventional and nuclear defense.

The importance of coupling was brought out in 1979, when it was decided to improve the theater nuclear posture and to couple the

U.S. strategic deterrent to the defense of Europe more securely by deploying nuclear-armed, ground-launched cruise missiles and the extended-range Pershing II ballistic missiles in Europe. That decision, by the way, was made in response to an increasing *nuclear threat* against Western Europe, not a conventional threat. It was a response to the new Soviet SS-20 mobile missile and the Backfire bomber and the rapidly growing theater nuclear capability of the Warsaw Pact that they represented, not to its conventional capability. After the SALT II debate, the need for some new symbol of the coupling of the United States to Europe was felt very strongly, especially in Germany. The only thing that would meet this need, it seemed, would be land-based missiles owned by the United States and deployed in Western Europe, with a range that could reach the Soviet Union.

Similarly, the present first-use posture, according to the four Germans, couples the U.S. nuclear deterrent to the conventional defense of Europe in a way that nothing else could. To abandon that and try to substitute an enhanced conventional defense for "deliberate escalation" would be politically, economically, and militarily unfeasible, they argue. For a start, they point out, Britain and America might have to reinstate the draft.

Finally, in direct opposition to their American counterparts, the four Germans argue that a no-first-use pledge would invite war.

Other notable Americans have also argued against dependence on first use. Herman Kahn, shortly before his death in 1983, wrote in the *New York Times* that we ought to be moving toward a no-first-use policy for NATO together with a buildup of conventional defenses. Three years earlier, Fred Iklé, before he became U.S. undersecretary of defense for policy, had an article in *Strategic Review* entitled "NATO's Nuclear First Use: A Deepening Trap?"[5] He virtually suggested that NATO ought as rapidly as possible to abandon reliance on first use, because it was trapping itself in a situation where it was likely to invite war, and it was likely to lose.

ALTERNATIVES TO FIRST USE

What is the possible response to this pressure to move NATO more and more into a posture of no first use? What are the alternatives?

General Bernard W. Rogers, NATO's supreme allied commander in Europe, has campaigned for raising the nuclear threshold by adopting new non-nuclear technologies that can take over a role in NATO that had previously been nuclear.[6] General Rogers argues that three improvements are urgently needed in NATO forces: (1) to correct long recognized deficiencies and improve the readiness of existing forces; (2) to continue the modernization begun in 1977-78; and (3) to move rapidly toward conventionalizing a previous tactical nuclear role, namely, that of defeating the "follow-on" ground forces (i.e., the immediate reinforcements) of the Warsaw Pact. This can be done—so argues General Rogers—by attack into Pact territory with the aid of new target-acquisition systems, improved command-control-communications, and new and improved non-nuclear munitions.

A study of European security published in 1983 under the auspices of the American Academy of Arts and Sciences came to similar conclusions.[7] Prepared by twenty-seven distinguished Americans and Europeans, this study examined the prospects for strengthening conventional defenses in Europe and decreasing dependence on nuclear weapons. It too relies heavily on advanced technologies—together with increased defense spending—for strengthening conventional capabilities in five critical mission areas: (1) to counter an initial Warsaw Pact ground attack; (2) to erode the enemy's air power; (3) to interdict and hold at risk his follow-on forces; (4) to disrupt or destroy his command, control, and communications; and (5) to secure reliable and effective NATO command and control. The aim is to achieve "conventional deterrence" as well as conventional defense.

Problems With a Conventional Balance

Neither General Rogers nor the European security study advocates a no-first-use pledge. Clearly, their purpose is to raise the nuclear threshold by exploiting some new opportunities for a conventional defense. Many others, including influential legislators such as Senator Sam Nunn, have joined in the enthusiasm for strengthening conventional defense by exotic technological means.

A number of Europeans have pointed out that such a path could lead to a situation that would not look very advantageous to Europeans. I agree with them, and am unsure that it would be greatly advantageous from an American point of view either. If we develop a genuine conventional balance, then Western Europe may face a greater possibility of a protracted conventional war on European soil, which has been the terrible fear for Europeans throughout the post-war years. I recall vividly the reactions of many Europeans while I was living in Germany in 1975 when I asked them about strengthening conventional defenses: "We don't want another Thirty Years' War in Europe."

For myself, I see nothing to be gained by a posture that might end up destroying Europe while "defending" it by conventional means in a protracted war. Nor do I believe that the new array of technologies offers any truly promising ways to disrupt a Warsaw Pact attack with conventional means so decisively as with nuclear means or to create the possibility of terminating a war.

Moreover, the idea of seeking a conventional balance raises such old issues as trading space for time and abandoning the forward defense concept. It also raises the possibility of deep counteroffensives into Eastern Europe.

Harvard professor Samuel Huntington, an advisor to U.S. administrations, has proposed that not only should we strengthen conventional direct defense capability but, if we really want to minimize dependence on nuclear weapons, we should also move to a new concept of a *conventional deterrent*, by which he means a conventional retaliatory capability.[8] What would such a capability be? According to Professor Huntington, it would be the capability, for example, to go into Eastern Europe and liberate Poland, or at least to threaten to liberate Poland. He is arguing that we should have the conventional capability to do retaliatory damage to the Soviet Union where it would hurt most—in its Eastern European empire.

In my own view, that road is treacherous. Following it would invite political tension such as we haven't seen for a long time. A continued reliance on nuclear weapons would be far preferable.

First Use: The Need to Decide

Mr. McNamara is quite right in his 1983 article in presenting this challenge: Do we or do we not want a posture of potential first use of nuclear weapons to deal with a conventional attack in Western

Europe? In settling that issue, we have to ask ourselves some very critical questions.

One of these is, Can we conceive of ways to use nuclear weapons in response to Soviet aggression with conventional forces that would be beneficial to NATO? McNamara says we have not achieved that conception yet. I suggest that there are some ways, but that we have not given sufficient attention to thinking them through and arriving at a convincing concept. If blame for this neglect is to be cast anywhere, some must go to Europe and some to the United States.

Many Europeans don't want to get explicit about situations in which nuclear weapons might be used because they think that deterrence depends upon uncertainty and ambiguity. The deterrent value of uncertainty and ambiguity has been grossly overrated, however. If you do not have a credible, reasonable response that your adversary believes you would invoke, you do not have a deterrent. Some American ways of answering McNamara's question, on the other hand, have sounded as if they would uncouple the defense of Europe from the U.S. strategic deterrent. They should be rejected for that reason.

If we cannot conceive of a beneficial use of nuclear weapons, and if we believe it unlikely that a U.S. president would authorize their use in the early hours of an East-West conflict, should we continue to accept the risks of basing NATO strategic war plans and nuclear weapons deployment on the assumption that the weapons *would* be used in such a situation? If not, what is the alternative posture?

Let us accept the challenge of Mr. McNamara and other opponents of a first-use posture head on. We have been intimidated too much and too long from critically and soberly discussing controlled and limited uses of nuclear weapons, both to deter a conventional attack and to extend deterrence into wartime should it fail to prevent the initial attack.[10]

None of the alternatives to a first-use posture of deterrence by controlled and limited nuclear means appears preferable. I reject massive retaliation and its variants of "assured destruction" on both ethical and strategic grounds. Conventional-only postures— while offering no convincing superiority on ethical or strategic grounds—do not seem to be technically feasible, economically affordable, or politically stabilizing.

In rejecting these alternatives, it is not necessary to press for a new "nuclear-emphasis" strategy for NATO. All parts of NATO's triad of capabilities—strategic nuclear, tactical nuclear, and conventional—are necessary to preserve each of NATO's options under the flexible response strategy: direct defense, deliberate escalation, and a general nuclear response. The capability to implement any one of the options makes both of the other two more viable and greatly enhances deterrence of aggression and our ability to preserve peace.

Christian Morality and
Nuclear Arms

EDWARD R. NORMAN

T HE CASE AGAINST nuclear weapons appears to be that they are different in scale and longevity of effect from other weapons. Christians who are not pacifists—who belong, that is, to the mainstream understanding of Christianity—ask themselves if the consequences of the use of nuclear weapons would be worse for human society than the evils that the weapons were intended to eradicate. For although deterrence remains the central hope of all concerned with the nuclear question, the very concept of deterrence requires a real intention to resort to nuclear arms should the need arise— that is, should an opponent initiate hostile military action that could be contained by no other means. Moreover, although deterrence has served mankind well for forty years, there is nothing in the human record to suggest that the priority of reason over emotion that currently preserves nuclear stability is likely to endure for all time. Christian thinkers must therefore go beyond deterrence to contemplate the morality of nuclear warfare itself.

Christianity is a historical religion, committed to history by God's intervention in historical processes: the rescue of the Jewish people and the military struggles that gave them a homeland, the material obligations attached to their covenant with God, the incarnation of God in Christ. In the Christian view of the world, men and women encounter not only God's nature but man's also as they take part in the material life of human society. Despite its noble ascetic tradition, Christianity has typically been an activist religion, expressed in the real world of changing events.

Much of what is now called "liberation theology" goes to enormous lengths to emphasize this activism—and it is right to do so.

Edward R. Norman is the dean of Peterhouse college and a former lecturer in history at Cambridge University. He is an Anglican priest and has written widely on church history and on ethical and political topics.

What is dubious about that school of thought is not its understanding of Christianity but its identification of Christianity with secular political ideology—an ideology that, moreover, is deeply materialistic and regards man's material condition as more important than the values he espouses. Traditional Christianity, though committed to the world, has sought to convert material conflicts into spiritual opportunities. It has tried, not to change the world (as the Marxists set out to do), but to redeem it. Salvation is more important than life; ultimate values are what really count.

Two Views of Human Nature

Through centuries of involvement with the world, both through the individual lives of believers and through connections between the church and human institutions, including the state, Christianity arrived at a developed view of human nature. That view was in the end characterized by hope—the prospect of salvation, freely offered to all men. But it was a deeply pessimistic view of the nature of man. Men in and of themselves were considered incapable of moral improvement, incapable of obtaining goodness through material means, and liable to ignore or distort their own spiritual capacities.

I put all this in the past tense because in recent years the Church has largely abandoned this view of human nature. In a surprising acceptance of secular values, the Church has adopted instead a tempered optimism about mankind. Recent church pronouncements and theological writings appear to endorse the opinion that humanity can make itself better by material means and that the moral condition of human society is indeed improving. One consequence of this new optimism is that modern Christianity increasingly regards warfare as a kind of barbarous survival that will cease once the full light of reason falls upon human society. Men will then overcome former ways of thinking and acknowledge their common humanity. Never before, not even in the most pagan societies of antiquity, has the stature of man been considered so high.

But man's demonstrated ability to contrive technical revolutions in no way undermines the traditional Christian view of human nature. Human genius was always there, as a gift from God, who made man in his image; but it was always flawed by the imperfections in the fallen creation. Those capable of producing a masterpiece of art or technology could be gravely deficient in moral judgment and spiritual perception.

Why Men Fight

It was the inventiveness and genius of man, however, not his moral and spiritual deficiency, that led to conflict. In the recorded conflicts of the past, men went to war not because they were inherently aggressive but because they were inherently ideological. Pacifists assume that good ideas can overcome human aggression. But it is *ideas*, not some inherent biological impulse, that send men into battle. The twentieth century is the great age of ideas. Mass education, rising expectations for both meaningful lives and material rewards, the politicization of moral values—these have helped to make our age the age of ideology. Therefore, the prospect is for more, not less, human conflict in the years ahead. At present enough social leadership and hierarchical deference survive from the old order to hold things in check. This presumably will not last.

Traditional Christianity knew these things. It recognized that what made men fight was usually not mere greed but values, ideas. The history of the civilized world, Christianity saw, was a history of conflict to secure values against competitors. Some of these values were good, some evil, just as men's natures were a mixture of the divine and the demonic. Whatever the evil of conflict, it was preferable to the surrender of values, for God had entrusted values to mankind—the treasure was in earthen vessels—and preserving these values was what life was all about.

In the process, of course, a lot of the secular got mixed up with the sacred; a lot of the personal material inclinations of the leaders were passed off as values when they were not. But warfare as such was seen by traditional Christianity as a part of human life, a permanent reminder to men that they cannot do what they so much want to do, which is to domesticate the world and remove the hazards and the pain from human existence.

The Old Testament is a record of God's involvement with his people as they carried out his will, often through armed conflict. It describes a small, militant people who, by means of arms, enforced their ideological conviction that God had given them territory, and who actually destroyed many peoples who opposed them. Radical

Christian theologians of today, who are greatly given to ransacking the prophetic writings to find instances of social criticism that they can use against modern capitalism, always manage to ignore the historical framework of the Old Testament. One can see why: it is essentially a cosmic essay in divine sanction, in force deployed for the sake of righteousness.

The Christian View of Peace

Christianity has also the vocation of peace, of course. To some extent Christianity transcends the Old Testament view of involvement with material processes. Men are now saved by their personal response to grace, no longer as part of a collective covenant. They are called upon to "turn the other cheek"—to suffer for righteousness, and not to mete out the punitive retribution of the old law. They are to love their neighbor as themselves, according to the most individual of all the social requirements of the new covenant.

And yet all these new orientations of the faith were not intended to cancel out the need for collective action; they were to show the necessity for prior personal conviction and response. Religion still called upon believers to provide the social conditions in which it could flourish and be transmitted; they were still required to fight for righteousness in armed conflict; they were still obliged to translate individual love of neighbor into a larger concern for social and national groups.

So too with the Christian understanding of "peace." The peace of the New Testament is inward, individual peace: the peace of the heart and the interior life, achieved by each believer himself in the face of worldly turmoil. This is one of the many paradoxes of Christianity (which showed its pedigree as a religion of the ancient world by its paradoxes—the poverty that was riches, the suffering that was exultation, the death that was life, the God who was man). Peace, in the Christian sense, is attained in the midst of the ever present conflict. It is the interior serenity of one whose priorities are beyond the reach of worldly sanction. What it is not is peace between nations or between those of conflicting ideologies. In fact, the Savior predicted warfare until the end of time.

Christians certainly have an obligation to seek peace with their neighbors, and they believe that this will project itself in the larger peace of societies. But they should be realistic enough to know that

worldly peace is incompatible with the pursuit of righteousness—
that man will be locked in a conflict of ideologies, in what he will
see as a conflict of good and evil, until the end.

The Scale of Destruction

This rather extensive survey seems to me an essential prerequi-
site to consideration of my initial point. What I have tried to show
is that Christians have traditionally regarded armed conflict as
inseparable from the facts of human nature—that it is man's very
genius at ideas that produces warfare, within the context of corrupted and fallen humanity. Weapons are only as evil as the people
who use them. If all the nuclear devices in existence were deto-
nated, there is a chance that most of life on earth would be destroyed
or transformed. But if all the swords in the ancient world had been
used at once to kill all opponents, a comparable effect would have
been produced. In both cases, reality is different from the extreme
model.

What is envisaged in a nuclear conflict is the destruction of large
areas of the industrial northern hemisphere; most of mankind would
be unaffected. Indeed, at the 1983 Assembly of the World Council
of Churches, leaders from the developing world took the Western
churches to task for becoming preoccupied with the peace movement—precisely because that was a matter that really concerned
only the developed nations.

Christians who object to nuclear weapons do so because they
cannot believe that destruction on so large a scale is a justifiable
means for preserving values. But is the scale really new? It is true
that in the past few centuries warfare in the West has been excep-
tionally limited in its effects. It has also been very expensive, a
sanction whose contemporary effects have only just begun to show.
But in the Middle Ages and in the ancient world—as among prim-
itive peoples everywhere—warfare tended to be total, and weapons
were used as destructively as their design would allow. Whole
civilizations were eliminated, whole peoples wiped out. Ancient
men were used to the idea that warfare was total, that to lose was
to face not merely personal annihilation but the actual destruction
of the society and the values it incorporated. Since whole towns
and cities were laid waste, crops were carried off, and fields were
burned, the long-term effects of such warfare were enormous—in

fact, they must have been very like those contemplated in nuclear warfare.

This highly destructive warfare was familiar to the Jewish historical tradition, and it was this conception of warfare that Christians inherited. When they accepted the need to defend values by armed conflict, they accepted the fact that the stakes were extremely high, and that total destruction of whole societies was a possible outcome. It is difficult and distasteful for us to accept this, accustomed as we are to the Western sense of security and of the "sanctity" of life.

Is Human Life 'Sacred'?

In readjusting to the idea of fighting for values at high cost—a permanent feature of civilized human life, whether we like it or not—we need to look rather closely at exactly what we mean by the "sanctity of human life." It is an ancient pagan concept that has undergone a modern revival. The phrase is commonly used, by Christians as well as by secular humanists, to describe a commitment to individual survival. But there is nothing very "sacred" about human beings: we are corrupted and in need of redemption. It is not human life but God who is sacred—and God has given us life in a "sacred" trust. No one should take away that life unless he does God's work of righteousness, as he understands it. Hence: "Thou shalt do no murder." But the preservation of values by armed conflict against militant opposition is not murder.

The morality is not altered by scale. The pursuit of values at great personal sacrifice, even at the cost of life itself, has always been thought to ennoble man. Heroic literature, as well as the sacred literature of past civilizations, abounds with examples. The saintly man may acquire virtue by turning the other cheek in a personal matter, where he forfeits the opportunity of revenge or gain by doing so; but in the collective defense of essential values he cannot behave in that way, for the result would be not personal but social. The defenseless and the children would lose the opportunity of practicing or being nurtured in values whose eternal importance transcends the value of individual human lives.

Such a version of things is now widely denigrated within liberal and educated opinion in the Western world. An exception is the socialist camp, where personal sacrifice for values is still held in high esteem, and where survival and extension of the ideology is regarded as enormously more important than the fate of present generations. It is one of the ways in which socialist societies are old-fashioned.

Force in Defense of Values

Despite the articulate adherence of the newly educated classes of the Western world to ideological positions—on human rights, democracy, and racial or sexual equality, for example—there is a general reluctance to use force to defend them. As in classic models of appeasement policy, a speciously "informed" view is put forth: countries being subverted in line with the "domino theory" are said to be ousting a corrupt government; there must be "negotiations," even with those who in their prior use of force have shown little regard for negotiated agreements; warfare is an "obscenity," a barbarous survival that no civilized person should contemplate.

But in the right circumstances, those given to attitudes such as these would urge the use of force to protect their own ideological presuppositions. Nothing so far indicates any widespread inner reconstruction of man. The twentieth century has been the great age of progressive enlightenment. It followed a century whose grossest departure from common sense was the supposition that education made people better morally, or at least more capable of reasoned moral choice. Yet the twentieth century has seen, and is still seeing, the deaths of countless millions for ideological reasons. Our generation is not in a good position to assert that men can control their emotions by reason. Those Christians who regard the defense of their values by force as wrong are closing their eyes to reality.

The most serious difficulty, however, is that these Christians are not really certain what their own essential values are. Defending God's laws on earth by physical means was perfectly satisfactory when it seemed possible to discern the Divine Will and to trust the scriptural record. But during the past century the leaders of Western Christianity have gradually withdrawn from many of the certainties of revealed knowledge, a withdrawal that in recent decades has become something of a stampede. They have also secularized the content of Christianity by readopting, as its moral core, a humanist view of man. It is an optimistic view, in which men and women are capable of achieving a measure of moral autonomy and of improving human life by material means. Love of neighbor is thought to require greater concern for people's material welfare than for the spirit in which they live. In the developing world, this means supporting socialist revolutionary movements on the grounds that they will give food and education to the people, whereas the old regimes, while they may have cultivated Christian belief, attended too little to material welfare. Often there is a deception in all this, and the same Christians who first spoke of the priority of material welfare are later found involved in the reeducation of the masses into ideology—into socialist ideology.

A Materialistic View of the Faith

A cause for concern is that some of the most influential Christians of the day now have a very materialistic view of the purpose of the faith. Witness the speeches made at the 1983 meeting of the World Council of Churches in Vancouver. Such a version of Christianity is unlikely to contemplate the defense of values at a high human cost precisely because it is unable to give a convincing eternal pedigree to its values. On top of that, the progressive political outlook of many Christian leaders today makes them unhappy about using weapons of mass destruction against the progenitors of ideologies that are not all that different from their own. Thus a changed view of the nature of man himself, and a consequent change in the orientation of Christian understanding, lie behind the increasing hostility of Christian groups in the West to the existence of nuclear arms.

Since the thinking of Western church leaders on these questions is closely related to the thinking of the liberal intelligentsia, there is little prospect of change unless there is a change within the wider community of thought. I do not believe, for example, that the 1983 vote by the General Synod of the Church of England to reject a motion for unilateral nuclear disarmament was particularly significant, except to show that the Synod, depicted for weeks beforehand in the English press as the slave of progressive fashion, decided on a demonstration of independence. At the same session it called upon Western governments to forswear first use of nuclear weapons, thereby (though they seem unaware of this) removing the flexible element in the deterrence strategy that gives it credibility.

I believe the central bodies of the major Western churches will continue their present drift towards advocating unilateral nuclear disarmament as long as the intelligentsia in general espouses unilateralism. A return by church leaders to traditional Christian doctrine might bring about a change, for religious certainty about revealed eternal truths would furnish ultimate values more dear than material welfare in this life. But there is no sign that any such shift is taking place; the movement is in the opposite direction.

The Churches as a Destabilizing Force

A hard and depressing conclusion, but one that seems unavoidable, is that the churches must be regarded for the immediate future as one of the forces making for destabilization of Western interests. Listen again to the speeches at the World Council of Churches' Vancouver Assembly and to the assent apparently given to even the most hostile anti-Western sentiments made in the name of humanity by respected Western church leaders.

The survival of human societies depends not upon the elimination of the bomb but upon ourselves. What Christians should be doing in the present debate about nuclear weapons is offering a view of the nature of man, of his enormous propensity for evil, and of the divine hope of goodness. Instead, they appear locked in a debate whose terms of reference, and whose views of human capability, seem almost entirely determined by secular thinking.

Christianity is called to be a peacemaker on earth. I have suggested that the true "peace" of Christianity is an interior serenity; yet the command of love of neighbor extends to a universal obligation not to seek his annihilation. Christians should be those whose knowledge of human fallibility best qualifies them to point out to parties engaged in dispute the emotional and selfish aspects of their claims.

Just as the Savior himself predicted strife for all time, so realistic Christians will recognize that there are some situations—rather frequently encountered too—where peaceful compromises and statesmanlike accommodations of opposed claims just will not hold. People who really believe in their values are unlikely to compromise them very greatly, and if they suppose that others are set upon the destruction of those values, no paper accommodation of differences will work. That is why pacifism is so unreal. It is also antisocial, since it leaves to others the dreadful task of protecting society against human evil in the only way that it can ever in the end be done—by sanction, by force.

Most of the great historical changes have occurred through force of arms, and the future is unlikely to be any different in this respect. As long as the deterrence thesis holds, that force may have limited effects. Christians should be realistic about the facts of human life, and should not high-mindedly insist upon negotiation of all disputes when they know that many of them will not be settled in that way. Love of neighbor certainly impels Christians to seek peace first, but not at the cost of essential values, or through the sacrifice of populations that would be left undefended in the face of human evil should the required force be unavailable.

The Churches' Great Opportunity

The stakes are now very high. The churches have been offered a great opportunity—which alas they show every sign of missing— to speak to man about his real nature. The existence of nuclear weapons poses a fearful threat to the human race, but it is the more fearful for those whose treasure is not in heaven.

To sum up: for Christians the major decision is now, as it has always been, whether it is proper to defend values by force—to kill other people in order to preserve what is regarded as truth. Once that decision has been made, as it has overwhelmingly in the past, in favor of the use of force in the appropriate circumstances, then the enormous destructive potential of nuclear weapons does not add anything new. Christians will of course seek to preserve the world from nuclear warfare, as from all occasions where brother kills brother, and to this end deterrence would seem to have proven advantages. But deterrence is an interim expedient, and the possibility of an actual resort to nuclear conflict will always remain. It is the duty of Christians to face that prospect clearly and to decide about its morality.

The Christian bodies that have continued to endorse a strategy of deterrence have tended at the same time to declare the *use* of nuclear weapons morally indefensible in all circumstances. But that will not do. Deterrence may one day break down; it implies use should need arise.The morality of deterrence is the same as the morality of use. This sort of realism, once characteristic of the Christian tradition, is quite compatible with an abhorrence of warfare of any sort.

Today, a recovery of Christian realism is indispensable if we are to have any hope of dealing properly with the moral problems posed by nuclear weapons.

Notes

Chapter Six: J. BRYAN HEHIR

1. National Conference of Catholic Bishops (U.S.A.), *The Challenge of Peace: God's Promise and Our Response*, A Pastoral Letter on War and Peace (Washington: U.S. Catholic Conference, 1983).

2. McGeorge Bundy, George F. Kennan, Robert S. McNamara, and Gerard K. Smith, "Nuclear Weapons and the Atlantic Alliance," *Foreign Affairs*, vol. 60, no. 4 (Spring 1982), pp. 753-68.

3. The Scowcroft Commission, with General Brent Scowcroft as chairman, was a bipartisan group set up in 1982-83 to advise on future ICBM policy. The MX missile was originally designed to remove the threat of a preemptive first strike against U.S. land-based missiles. MX missiles were to be deployed in a widespread mobile network. However, this plan appeared to be too expensive, and the commission recommended deployment of 100 MX missiles in existing silos. It also recommended the deployment of smaller ICBMs that could be launched from silos or mobile carriers.

4. MIRV: Multiple Independently-targetable Reentry Vehicle, by which a number of nuclear warheads are dispatched from one launcher-rocket, each warhead then being guided to a separate target.

Chapter Seven: MICHAEL NOVAK

1. Aleksandr Solzhenitsyn, *Warning to the West* (New York: Farrar, Straus and Giroux, 1976), pp. 76-77.

2. Details of force strength may be found in *The Military Balance 1984-1985* (London: The International Institute for Strategic Studies, 1984); U.S. Department of Defense, *Soviet Military Power*, second edition (Washington, D.C.: U.S. Government Printing Office, 1983); and Michael B. Donley, ed., *The SALT Handbook* (Washington, D.C.: The Heritage Foundation, 1979).

3. Salvador de Madariaga, chairman of the League of Nations Disarmament Conference, speaking in 1973. Quoted in Barbara W. Tuchman, "The Alternative to Arms Control," *New York Times Magazine* (April 18, 1982), p. 98. Miss Tuchman also writes after chronicling the various unsuccessful efforts at arms control: "I have engaged in this long and dreary survey in order to show that control of war in the form of disarmament or limitation of arms has been a fruitless effort" (p. 93).

4. Theodore Draper, "How Not to Think About Nuclear War," *New York Review of Books* (July 16, 1982), p. 42. Commenting on the celebrated no-first-use proposal of McGeorge Bundy, George F. Kennan, Robert S. McNamara, and

Gerard Smith (*Foreign Affairs*, Spring 1982), Draper adds: "If a declaration of peaceful intentions were enough to prevent any kind of war, the deed would have been done a long time ago. The history of war and peace is littered with such professions of virtue. In 1928, for example, sixty-two nations signed a pact outlawing war. Its enforcement was supposed to rest on the moral strength of world opinion. It was signed, celebrated, and forgotten. With evident understatement, the four authors themselves say that 'such declarations may have only limited reliability.' The awful truth is that they have no reliability at all" (p. 35).

5. Testimony of David A. Stockman, director, Office of Management and Budget, before the Joint Economic Committee, U.S. Congress, May 4, 1983.

6. For numbers of strategic bombers see Kevin N. Lewis, *The Economics of SALT Revisited* (Santa Monica, Calif.: Rand Corp., 1979), p. 13; and *The Military Balance 1984-1985*, pp. 4-5. Regarding the size of the U.S. nuclear arsenal, Secretary of Defense Caspar Weinberger notes: "We have fewer nuclear warheads today than we had in 1967—not a handful fewer but thousands fewer." See News Release No. 168-82 (20 April 1982), Office of Assistant Secretary of Defense (Public Affairs). Although the exact number of nuclear warheads is classified, a careful student can deduce that, while the number of strategic warheads has remained relatively steady, the number of tactical warheads has declined, resulting in an overall reduction in the totality of the U.S. stockpile since 1965. A chart prepared by the Harvard Nuclear Study Group shows that the throwweight of the U.S. strategic missile force has declined by half in the past decade and a half. See Albert Carnesale et al., *Living With Nuclear Weapons* (New York: Bantam Books, 1983), p. 103. See also the essay (and accompanying charts) by Sven F. Kraemer in the present volume, especially pages 19–24.

7. See Michael Charlton, "The Eagle and the Small Birds: The Spectre of Yalta," *Encounter*, June 1982, pp. 7-28.

8. At SALT I, U.S. negotiators concentrated on limiting launchers, which are easier to verify. Thus arose MIRVing, multiplying the number of warheads on each launcher. Thus does the search for objects easy to verify distort negotiations.

9. See Edward E. Ericson, Jr., *Solzhenitsyn: The Moral Vision* (Grand Rapids, Mich.: Eerdmans, 1980), p. 151.

Chapter Eight: FRANS A. M. ALTING VON GEUSAU

1. Charter 77 became known through a declaration issued on January 1977. It is an informal group of Czechoslovak citizens committed to defense of human rights and individual freedoms. Charter 77 is not an organization as such and does not express political opposition. It merely calls upon the government of Czechoslovakia to abide by international agreements it has accepted, such as the International Covenant on Civil and Political Rights, the Universal Declaration of Human Rights, and the Helsinki Final Act. Members of Chapter 77 have been harassed, persecuted, imprisoned, or expelled.

2. In "total foreign policy," a concept introduced by Lenin, diplomacy is a form of warfare using all available means—political, economic, cultural, psychological—to achieve the defeat of the adversary.

Chapter Nine: ROBERT A. GESSERT

1. The Committee on the Present Danger was founded in November 1976 to monitor the U.S.-Soviet military balance and arms-control proposals and negotiations. Its headquarters are in Washington, D.C.

2. Robert S. McNamara, "The Military Role of Nuclear Weapons," *Foreign Affairs*, vol. 62, no. 1 (Fall 1983), pp. 59-80.

3. McGeorge Bundy, George F. Kennan, Robert S. McNamara, and Gerard K. Smith, "Nuclear Weapons and the Atlantic Alliance," *Foreign Affairs*, vol. 60, no. 4 (Spring 1982), pp. 753-68.

4. Karl Kaiser, Georg Leber, Alois Mertes, and Franz-Josef Schulze, "Nuclear Weapons and the Preservation of Peace: A German Response," *Foreign Affairs*, vol. 60, no. 5 (Summer 1982), pp. 1157-70.

5. Fred Charles Iklé, "NATO's 'First Nuclear Use': A Deepening Trap?," *Strategic Review*, vol. VIII, no. 1 (Winter 1980), pp. 18-23.

6. See, for example, the following articles by General Rogers: "The Atlantic Alliance: Prescriptions for a Difficult Decade," *Foreign Affairs*, Summer 1982, pp. 1145-56. / "Embracing Deterrence—Raising the Nuclear Threshold," *NATO Review*, February 1983, pp. 6-9. / "Sword and Shield: ACE Attack of Warsaw Pact Follow-On Forces," *NATO's Sixteen Nations*, February-March 1983, pp. 16-26. / "ACE Attack of Warsaw Pact Follow-On Forces," *Military Technology*, May 1983, pp. 38-60. / "Greater Flexibility for NATO's Flexible Response," *Strategic Review*, Spring 1983, pp. 11-19.

7. Report of the European Security Study, *Strengthening Conventional Deterrence in Europe: Proposals for the 1980s* (New York: St. Martin's Press, 1983).

8. Samuel P. Huntington, "The Renewal of Strategy," in Huntington, ed., *The Strategic Imperative: New Policies for American Security* (Cambridge: Ballinger Press, 1982). See also Samuel P. Huntington, "Conventional Deterrence and Conventional Retaliation in Europe," unpublished manuscript prepared for the U.S. Army War College Strategic Studies Institute Conference on "Defense and Deterrence in the 1980s: New Realities—New Strategies," July 1983.

9. In March 1974, in his first annual report to the Congress on the defense budget and the defense program, then Secretary James R. Schlesinger called for a rational, national debate on limited and selective uses of nuclear weapons should initial deterrence fail. Unfortunately, we did not have much of a debate, as the few voices raised in support of limited, selective use were mostly drowned out by a flood of rhetoric in reassertion of the pernicious MAD (mutual assured destruction) doctrine. For one example, however, of a proposal for a controlled, limited, and selective first use of nuclear weapons in response to a Pact conventional attack on NATO, a use aimed at disrupting and disorganizing the attack in order to deter further aggression and terminate the conflict, see a monograph I prepared jointly with the second and former director of nuclear planning on the NATO International Staff: Robert A. Gessert and Harvey B. Seim, *Improving NATO's Theater Nuclear Posture: A Reassessment and a Proposal* (Washington, D.C.: Georgetown University, Center for Strategic and International Studies, 1977).

Bibliography

Ball, George W. *The Discipline of Power*. Boston: Little, Brown, 1968.

Dyson, Freeman. *Weapons and Hope*. New York: Harper and Row, 1984.

Ehrlich, Robert. *Waging Nuclear Peace: The Technology and Politics of Nuclear Weapons*. Albany, N.Y.: State University of New York, 1985.

Gray, Colin S. *Nuclear Strategy and Strategic Planning*. Philadelphia: Foreign Policy Research Institute, 1984.

Heller, Joseph. *Catch-22*. New York: Simon and Schuster, 1961.

Holloway, David. *The Soviet Union and the Arms Race*. New Haven: Yale University, 1983.

Jastrow, Robert. *How to Make Nuclear Weapons Obsolete*. Boston: Little, Brown, 1985.

Kirkpatrick, Jeane J. *We and They: Understanding Ourselves and Our Adversary*. Washington: Ethics and Public Policy Center, 1983.

Kissinger, Henry A. *White House Years*. Boston: Little, Brown, 1979.

Lefever, Ernest W., ed. *Nuclear Arms and Soviet Aims*. Essays by Ronald Reagan, Pierre Gallois and John Train, Eugene V. Rostow, and Paul H. Nitze. Washington: Ethics and Public Policy Center, 1984.

Lefever, Ernest W., and Hunt, E. Stephen, eds. *The Apocalyptic Premise: Nuclear Arms Debated*. Washington: Ethics and Public Policy Center, 1982.

MacIntyre, Alasdair. *After Virtue*. Notre Dame, Ind.: University of Notre Dame, 1981.

Military Balance, The. London: International Institute for Strategic Studies, annual.

National Conference of Catholic Bishops. *The Challenge of Peace: God's Promise and Our Response*. Washington: United States Catholic Conference, 1983.

Nixon, Richard. *Real Peace: A Strategy for the West*. N.p., 1983.

_____. *The Real War*. New York: Warner Books, 1980.

Novak, Michael. *Moral Clarity in the Nuclear Age*. Nashville: Thomas Nelson, 1983.

Olive, Marsha McGraw, and Porro, Jeffrey D., eds. *Nuclear Weapons in Europe: Modernization and Limitation*. Lexington, Mass.: Lexington Books, 1983.

127

Pannenberg, Wolfhart. *Human Nature, Election, and History*. Philadelphia: Westminster, 1977.

Schell, Jonathan. *The Fate of the Earth*. New York: Knopf, 1982.

Sigal, Leon V. *Nuclear Forces in Europe: Enduring Dilemmas, Present Prospects*. Washington: Brookings Institution, 1984.

Strategic Survey. London: International Institute for Strategic Studies, annual.

Vermaat, J. A. Emerson. *Moscow and the European Peace Movement*. Washington: Ethics and Public Policy Center, 1983; reprinted from *Problems of Communism*, November-December 1982.

Index of Names